A parrot in my soup....and other complaints

By

Andy Frazier

Other titles from this author

The Right Colour – a charming story about a cow on a mission.

I use my thumbs as a yardstick – a biography of some old bloke who did loads of stuff.

Princess the cow series (aimed at younger readers)

- *About a cow*
- *In the company of animals*
- *Cow Factor*
- *The Royal Detective*

Beales Corner – *a boy adventure story set in the little town of Bewdley during WW2*

First published March 2010
Lulu edition
ISBN 978-1-4478-2242-4

For more information visit www.andyfrazier.co.uk

Introduction

One day I woke and realised that I was pretty fed up with the world, or at least certain things in it. Yeah yeah, have a moan about it, why not, everyone else does? But I took my moaning a step further, I took it to ranting proportions. Then I wrote it down. Then lo and behold my scribblings were printed in a local monthly publication.

A couple of years have passed since that epiphany and I now have amassed quite a deluge of ranting in print. Most of them concern our life on a smallholding in France but sometimes I look a little further.

So this book is just that, a deluge of rantings. Read it and weep with me!

Index

Who am I?

The self confessed statement of "I grew up on a farm" is a condition that never leaves you: "you can take the man from the farm but never the farmer out from the man". And so, as a second son leaving the family farm in my late twenties and working my way through various agricultural careers, I eventually found myself involved in corporate business. I had an office in the city, commuted by train in a suit, rubbing shoulders with folks I neither knew, understood nor liked. I sometimes discussed with my peers the days gone by when I groomed champions, or flew a herd of cattle to Australia, but it only met with disbelief. Let's just say, what I was doing I did for the money. I connived to find time to still enjoy breeding and showing a few livestock but fitted it around a day job, as I raised my flocks of texel and hebredian sheep. I managed to keep an active involvement in a few major shows too and was even deputy chief cattle steward at Royal Smithfield show for a while. But I was never free.

I am not sure what exactly made me snap, but one day, the moment arrived for me to say enough is enough; I always knew it would come. What I was left with was unemployment alongside a bag full of memories, experiences many folk could never even dream of. That and a new life, to do with what I pleased.

What I pleased to *do* was to do less, and enjoy more. That is what drove me to buy a smallholding in

South Western France, with a big old house, 3 hectares of grassland and orchards, long sunny days and a woman I wanted to share it with. I now have only 4 sheep, one which has the horns of a Norfolk, the others just mediocre ewes serving a purpose. I collect the fruit to make preserves and this year hosted the first and highly successful Aquitaine chutney festival, a gathering of chutneyheads to compete for the coveted prize of *pickle of the year*. Although Wendy keeps a day job, we are more or less self sufficient. My summer days are busy with building and renovating the house and my winter days are busier still, filled with writing.

My first novel called on my experiences as a cattle stockman in search of that holy grail, supreme champion of the Royal Smithfield show. Seen through the eyes of the animal, it tells a unique tale of a calf overcoming adversity and setting out on a special journey towards her destiny. I was never exactly sure who would buy it, but buy it they have, and judging by the positive feedback I constantly receive, they have all enjoyed it, young and old. It is called the Right Colour.

From there I moved on to writing childrens stories. I had often sat and wondered what animals would say and do if they took on a few human characteristics. This led me to write the adventures of Princess, a young cow with attitude. Her adventures have now grown into a series of 5 books aimed at readers aged 9-12,, of which every one has been a thrill to write. I truly believe I have the best job in the world.

Courgettes and ex-pats
March 09.

Welcome to my first rantings from rural France. It will soon be 3 years since I left the British shores exchanging a life in and around Rock for a similar one in South West France. I tell a lie, it is nearly 3 years since I left UK, but I did spend 6 months in central Amsterdam, before settling, much to my children's disapproval, on a much quieter and more sedate life here in the France countryside. We do have a night club a few miles away I tell them when trying to encourage them to visit me, but seemingly it is not quite up to the nightlife hotspot of my old flat in the Liedseplein. Its certainly quieter I am glad to say, very few drunken hen parties wearing union jack outfits stagger down this road at 4am. Some, but very few.

So here we are, myself, my partner Wendy, 2 daft dogs, a plethora of cats and very little income on a 9 acre plot, an hour south of Bordeaux. Our local village of Puymiclan is a tad smaller than Rock, but does host a shop and a hairdressers, and more recently a restaurant. The latter opened last year to much fanfare, but sadly was closed by Xmas. It seems that George, the proprietor, with his inspired idea of regularly doubling his prices to make more money failed to comply with the general rules of commerce, as his client numbers dwindled to zero! But I have recently noticed that the signs are now up, and a new owner is about to launch his own particular ideas on the village, albeit we only have 500 residents. We await with baited garlic breath.

Wendy & I don't get out much and most of our socialising tends to be at home, either from the bbq or from my ever expanding "make-it-up-as-you-go-using-whats-in-the-fridge" cookbook. During winter I play pool for a local bar on Friday evenings, which is somewhat entertaining and involves some quite considerable travelling to far off similar bars. The competition is hot and both myself and our team are trailing near the bottom of the league table this season. Wendy rarely joins in, most bars here being not particularly women friendly and the nights are usually very late. We have an eclectic mix of friends, which I am sorry to say are mainly ex-pats, them being aplenty in the Dordogne. However, most of the British population here originate from south of Watford, which constitutes being a southerner in my book and should be treated with utmost suspicion!

Anyway, spring has finally arrived in Lot-et-Garronne, after what has been a tedious and cold winter. This year, due to the price of fuel, we decided to maintain our heating using only firewood which is relatively cheap here, especially if you get your own from the nearby wood! We have a huge fireplace that includes a huge chimney which I am convinced has some ingenious kind of vacuum cleaner in it, sucking all the heat from the room, and leaving us with just the smoke! Finally, after a visit from sister in January, during which the entire house froze solid, leaving us waterless for a week, we succumbed to buying some heating fuel to see us through the remaining winter months. Although the world price of fuel had decreased a little by this point, I am pretty sure our local bandit of a fuel merchant added 10% because it was so cold, and a further 10 because we are English! C'est la vie.

Springtime has always been my favourite time of year, the time for back-breaking gardening and repairing of garden machinery, not to mention the enjoyable spring sounds such as night-visiting tom cats and low flying aircraft. But at least we can venture outside now, in fact as a rule it is invariably warmer outside than in, as these old French houses are designed to stay cool in summer. If only they were designed to stay warm in winter, I think they may have been on to a winner. So it's planting les pomme-de-terre today in our extensive veg garden. I have to point out that I am no real gardener, but coming from farming stock, I thought "how hard can it be?" After months of toil on this heavy clay ground, I did manage to provide a few family meals last year, and we especially enjoyed courgette pie, courgette pate, courgette pickle and courgette custard! It wasn't until December that we had our annual water bill, the French water board advising us that the usual bill for this house was 150 euros, so perhaps this years bill of 450 euros may be due to a leak somewhere? No I replied, just me watering the veggies through May til September. Yes, it has been pointed out to me that our local supermarket supplies fabulous local vegetables, all at rock bottom prices whilst in season, and that a purchase of 300 euros from there would be so plentiful it may take a considerable amount of car journeys to collect. But surely that is not the point of gardening is it? It's about self sufficiency, and pride, and back pain. So we are back at it again. Perhaps a few less courgettes this year though, there's only so much courgette soup a body can endure!

Springtime

April 2009

Some of you may know that the Aquitaine region of France is renowned for its passion for the sport of rugby. With teams like Agen and Toulouse, they are not only passionate about it, but pretty damn good at it too. I will admit that rugby is also a life long obsession of my own and that it is no coincidence that we ended up living in this area.

So as you can imagine, the annual clash of England and Les Bleu is a much discussed topic around this time of year, and considered something of a battle.

Now I can vaguely remember having a conversation in a pub with a French fellow on the Friday prior to the match, and accepting a handshake during which the words "bet" and "drink" were uttered in French, and I had assumed this meant that next time we met one would owe the other a beer, depending on the result. So it was to my surprise that I opened the door at 9pm on Saturday to find this near stranger armed with no less than 6 bottles of wine, uttering the only English word he knew which was "normal". We only managed to drink 3 of the bottles while discussing the match before I fell asleep on the sofa and my new best friend departed. For all I know he may well re-appear next year. Needless to say, and for those of you who were unaware, England won the game by a big margin. Just as well, as I later found out that as is "normal" on such occasions, had we lost I was bound to visiting his house with similar wine stash of my own. I could be smug and suggest that since we have beaten France on the last 4 occasions that an ongoing tradition such as this may be becoming a little expensive for them, but one doesn't like to gloat. If only the Welsh were such good losers, surely Europe would be a better place! One thing I did gain from this experience is that my tendency to say "oui, oui" during French conversations to any sentence I cannot understand, probably needs reconsidering!

As our place used to be a tobacco farm, at the bottom of our field we have a small irrigation lake, which is now host to a menagerie of wildlife of varying shapes and sizes. These include a few hundred hungry carp, a well fed heron and some very active coypu whose main objective appears to be burrowing so much soil from the bank that I am terrified that one day the whole field will collapse, swallowing the lake and my Ford tractor in the process. But by far the most irritating are the million frogs (animal frogs, not the French peasants!) who at this time of year become extremely vocal during which I can only assume is the mating season. At first it was quite amusing to witness them taking turns to shout their monotone statements to each other across the pond, and Wendy assures me it is, as always, the male of the species doing all the talking. Well I am not so convinced by this and believe it is actually a female thing, in the same way that our she cats frequently yowl to summon the services of the omnipresent stray tom to our door each spring. I sometimes wonder if the frogettes (or whatever the correct term is for female frogs) are giggling, in the same way that a class of teenage girls may do in front of a young handsome teacher? Only very much louder. When I say the pond is at the bottom of the field, it is a good 2-300 metres from the house but still the frog symphony is so loud that it is virtually impossible to for us to sleep at night. I only wish my old housemaster could be here to administer his effective punishment for talking after lights out.

Whilst on the subject of stray tomcats, it appears that our first "litter" of kittens has arrived already and a muffled squeaking can be heard hailing from the attic. I use the word litter, as this is very much my general opinion of cats. However, this lot are in fact quite timely, as our annual house party is planned for next month and this year we are considering sending guests home with a party bag containing at least one kitten! Some may even get the jackpot and get a fully grown cat too, specifically the one who made off with my pork chops last week!

Now spring is officially here and the sun is shining brightly the time arrives to relieve our scruffy mongrel dog of her shaggy coat. As the local dog grooming parlour, known in French for some strange reason as a "toilettage", sees fit to charge a monarch's ransom for a shampoo and set, I decided to do the deed myself this year. Armed with noisy electric shears and a lifetimes experience of clipping cattle and shearing sheep, I engaged in the task. It didn't go well. In fact (pardon the pun) to cut a long story short, a half shaven, slightly bleeding bewildered mutt could occasionally be sighted, with the aid of very strong binoculars, seeking sanctuary amongst the giggling frogs for nigh on a week afterwards. On her eventual recapture the job was completed but immediately the weather reverted back to winter and then the poor thing wouldn't stop shivering. The word dog-coat was quickly mentioned and investigations were made to the nice lady at the toilettage whom as luck would have it also marketed a range of fashionable dog-wear, at fashion shop prices. Now some might say that Gucci-poochy wear may look fine at Crufts or even in Paris, but in my view it definitely wasn't right for our scruffy creature, no matter how bad her haircut was, so I stood my ground. Anyway, after a few days of minor domestic disagreements, eventually a usable article was "fashioned" from an old track-suit, which had previously been worn for painting. Problem is, now the scruffy dog looks even scruffier. In fact she wouldn't look out of place peering from a large cardboard box on Kidderminster high street in the early hours. Big Issue anyone?

The annual Soiree

May 2009

I mentioned last month about our rather noisy frogs, which thankfully have calmed down a little after my threat of selling their limbs to our local restaurant. Maybe their mating season has ended or perhaps they just do it quietly after shouting about it for a month beforehand, who knows.

But we now have a new irritant. At first it arrived on our bird table one day, a more beautiful creature it would be hard to imagine, light red body, black and white stripy wings, an orange hat and grey crest on its head that apparently only rises to the vertical when it is annoyed, as it evidently was. We know all this through Google, which informs us that it is imaginatively named as the Hoopoe bird. I say imaginatively named as for the past 3 weeks it sits on our roof calling its mate. "Hoop hoop" its says, "hoop hoop hoop" she replies. Now one would assume he is saying "you look nice today dear, I particularly like the hat", and she may reply "not so shabby yourself big boy". So why oh why does he keep saying the same thing, over and over and over, 18 hours a day, starting at daylight?! It's maddening. I believe if Sky TV made a program entitled "The worlds top 100 most irritating creatures", Hoopy would be there at number one, possibly narrowly beating Germaine Greer into second place.

We held our annual party last week to celebrate our being together for 3 years, and our 2 years in this French farmhouse. A 40-strong eclectic mix of people turned up during the day for barbequing and general frolicking. Our invite was worded "1 o'clock onwards", which unfortunately doesn't translate into French very well, so our neighbouring farmer appeared, washed for once, in his best clothes at one minute past, along with his wife and daughter. At this time, our close friends and house guests were still scurrying round moving tables and mopping floors etc, and I think Farmer Eric was a little embarrassed that he had arrived a lot earlier than any other guest. However, as farmers do, he was prepared to roll up his sleeves and join in the last minute tidying up, but from her expression I think his wife drew the line at that and they shortly departed, her using words I am rather glad I could not understand. They didn't return.

The Sunday morning after the event was the usual carnage of empties and broken furniture as the overnight guests gradually emerged for breakfast. I will admit I was quite surprised to also see a pair of well dressed gentlemen whom I did not recognise appearing on the drive, carrying a large book. I wearily realised that they were men of the cloth, or at least staunch followers and touring preachers of the good words from "le Bon Libre". I had a short conversation with them in French, me in my dressing gown and hangover, and mentioned that maybe some of my house guests were indeed in need of redemption. I am guessing that as I lead them round to the breakfast table on the rear terrace, through a sea of empty bottles, the pair of them realised that maybe this was a lost cause, but they still persevered and arrived on the top steps with the Good Book open and ready. I will admit, I have never seen so many people scarper with such thin excuses in all my life. The best one being my 'sisters' "I haven't got time for redemption, I have to go and do the washing up!". I am ashamed to admit that the sermon was delivered in French to myself, one uninterested scruffy dog (now without her coat) and to the stereo accompaniment of 2 hoopoe birds telling each other how nice they look. I was not fast enough to translate all of it but I believe it was something to do with "some falling on stony ground".

In our small lake we have a lot of fish, probably around 400 of them. I am told by someone I met in a pub that they are a type of carp and they like to eat bread. So for the last 12 months all our stale bread gets thrown to them each evening. They arrive in shoals like piranha and gobble it up with a horrible sucking sound, often aided by our Pointer dog who swims after every crumb like some kind of crazed "PACMAN"! When my son came to stay recently, he suggested we went fishing so we reluctantly purchased a fishing rod, needless to say without the slightest real clue of what to do with it. "It's easy" I guessed, just put bread on the hook, no problem. To be honest I was concerned he may catch so many fish with each cast that we would have to abandon after 30 minutes for fear of emptying the entire contents of the lake. Not so. The canny creatures can manage to eat all the bread from the hook without actually taking a hook itself. I am sure there are carp fishing experts out there, but we had none on hand amongst our friends and guests. Try sweetcorn one said, they love Spam another offered, but all was in vain. So it was back to Google who informed us that they like fragrant foods such as fruity things and stilton cheese, but as we were fresh out of fruitgums or Roquefort we still had no ammo. I did suggest that we do have a large net that we use to clean the swimming pool or possibly some explosives in the poly-tunnel but seemingly this would be cheating. Anyway, after reverting once more back to stale bread, he did retrieve one poor slippery example, photographed it and returned it again.

Over the last few months we have spotted one extraordinary large fish, and some wag has nicknamed it "the Colonel". It seems that I have now been commissioned to catch said beast in some kind of family wager. He doesn't really look appetising with new potatoes, so I cannot actually see the point of this, but I suppose I have to keep face. So now maybe 'its time to consult the local experts, or possibly to get creative with my PC and some photo editing software! See next month for photos..!

Blondes on my shoes

June 2009

Last weekend saw the opening of all the summer festivals of culture in South West France. We slipped over the border into the Gironde region who started their season with a free concert with none other than Birmingham's own UB40. It was particularly entertaining to hear 3000 French students singing along to "there's a rat in the kitchen, what am I gonna do…" and I remember thinking that I couldn't recall any French bands ever having produced gems such as that! Come to think of it, it's my belief that France is pretty incapable of producing music at all. Let's face it, this is a nation that gave us Charles Aznavour, Sacha Distel and Plastic Bertrand (and even he was half Belgian). All totally unforgivable in my book. OK they also gave us Jean-Michel Jarre and the great Edith, but there the list ends. No doubt someone will be keen to point out that France did come 8th in this years Eurovision song contest. I rest my case M'Lud!

During most of the year our main staple diet here is wine and potatoes. The latter home grown and the former collected from the local wine cooperative in our own containers for which the price has increased this year to just over £1 per litre for the regular, and £1.50 for 4 star. Mostly we opt for the better stuff, but always keep a supply of 2 star on hand for visitors! However, as many will know, Bordeaux is world famous for its red wine, our nearest decent vineyards being at St.

Emilion just 30 minutes away which is a fabulously wealthy little town full of wine caves and chic bistros, all grossly over priced for the tourists. For the wine bores amongst you, the greater vineyards on the Haut Medoc such as Pauillac, Graves & Margaux are also within our reach geographically, but sadly not financially. We grow most of our own vegetables as mentioned earlier, and share them with a variety of other creatures including brightly coloured slugs, bugs, beetles and birds. We pride ourselves that we rarely open cellophane packets and I not sure we even possess a tin opener. We also have an assortment of fruit trees including lemons, peaches and hopefully kiwi fruit, the latter being widely commercially grown in this region. I say hopefully, as we have discovered that the kiwi has male and female plants, which I suppose fits in well with similar traits in the French language. I am reliably informed (by a bloke I met in the pub) that one male plant can look after up to 5 females. This French conversation was then turned into a joke followed by much laughter, the gist of which I understood but based on a previous experience I kept silent this time. Well we have two very large kiwi plants which have yet to bear us fruit, but this year are at least displaying multiple flowers. Problem is I am unsure which, if either, is a female or how your can even establish this fact. Moreover I have no idea how they are cross pollinated or whatever the correct term is for plants copulating. So we could have 50kgs of kiwis, or just a lot of impotent male flowers. We can only wait and see.

Anyway, I recently extended our terrace on the North side of the house to include a couple of work units and a gas hob, so for 8 months a year our alfresco living involves grabbing handfuls of fresh herbs such as basil, coriander and tarragon into a wok to make sauces for whatever we have in the freezer for this month. We did make a gallant attempt at producing our own lamb, based on my reasonable experience of sheep breeding but sadly our 6 pedigree ewes were killed by stray dogs last year. It was a tough day, and one we would rather forget.

Having earned my living for many years in the pedigree livestock industry I have worked just about every breed of cattle on the planet, and I have to say the my least favourite was the Blonde d'Aquitaine. They are huge animals with long legs that can kick like Johnny Wilkinson and run like Usain Bolt, and have attitude to match *Iron* Mike Tyson himself. I can vividly recall many years ago having the job of taming a French cow called 'Volcano' and a more aptly named beast I have yet to encounter. At 3 years old, she was already with her 4th owner, never a good sign. We did manage to get her to the Royal Show but to this day I still bear the scars. As the name suggests, Blondes originally hail from the Aquitaine region of France, and thus they now surround us. Everywhere I look I get reminded of that fateful day at Kenilworth and my shoulder starts to twinge. But by far the worst aspect of these angry creatures is the texture of the meat that they provide, which is nothing other than ghastly. As they contain little or no fat, it is unadvisable to hang the meat for any length of time or else it will blacken. Combine this with the fact that the animals are not slaughtered until 3 years old, and you end up with reams of inedible red meat that at best is un-chewable and at worst usable only to re-sole my Grensons! My neighbour Eric, he with the disapproving wife, takes delight in presenting us with some pedigree beef as part payment for using our hay field. I assure you pedigree chum would be far more welcome. One day I will visit him with some Aberdeen Angus steak, and hopefully he will get the message. If I was considering a new profession in this area I would definitely opt for dentistry!

One of the attractions of the Lot et Garonne region of France is the fact that it is always very green and lush compared to regions further south. The reason for this is the incredible thunderstorms we endure during the summer months which come in off the Atlantic. These often include spectacular pyrotechnic sky displays to rival those of Bastille Day but they are unfortunately extremely unpredictable.

On many an evening, with glass in hand, we can be sitting out, bbq aglow, eagerly awaiting our forthcoming gastronomic experiment when without warning the heavens open and literally put a dampener on proceedings. This is generally 2 minutes before the "chicken surprise" is cooked and 5 minutes after I have just invested 5 euros in watering the vegetable patch. To be fair, they are usually preceded by a swift gust of wind which scatters table napkins around the garden in some kind of 1 minute warning and thus we have honed the skill of retreat-to-eat. Still I suppose this inconvenience is a small price to pay for the incredible colour that adorns our garden through the summer months. Right now everything is in flower including the spuds, tomatoes, geraniums and the very attractive Oleander bushes which sport deep red flowers all summer. One other beauty is the Cala Lilly which grows wild here often in huge clumps on the side of the road. I recently realised that I really should be gathering these and sending them in van loads back to UK where a small *hand* tied bunch from Interflora, according to their website, will set you back upwards of £50! Comforting to know they would be "hand-tied" I suppose. As apposed to what I am not sure, tied by feet or teeth perhaps? Maybe tied by robots using pliers, who knows? For my sins I once worked in marketing but it still amazes me what they can get away with!

Continuing with my fishy story from last month, my friend's father-in-law visited us last week to give some fishing advice. This guy is the equivalent of a double-dan black-belt in fishing, and what he doesn't know about carp fishing etc etc…. So with something over a grand's worth of complicated kit and bait from a closely guarded secret recipe he set about tempting the "Colonel" on to dry land while we waited with silent anticipation. Ha, not a chance! In fact in 2 hours I don't think he caught anything bigger than a sardine. My son had caught bigger ones last time with the rod we bought for a fiver at the filling station. The big fella is certainly becoming a challenge. I think capturing the Loch Ness monster might be easier, or possibly finding Nemo!

Michelin men and flying flip-flops

July 2009

As with UK this summer has been one of extremes, seeing temperatures up near 40 degrees which is starting to get too hot even for me, let alone the animals and plants. To much distress a short while ago I noticed the beginnings of blight in the tomatoes which any gardener will tell you should be prevented and is not really curable. Well fortunately we had a long dry spell after that, probably 4 weeks without rain, so with the aid of my sprayer and "Bordeaux mixture" (a potent concoction of copper sulphate & lime) I had managed to contain the disease, hoping to preserve the crop of upwards of 30kgs of green tomatoes at least through to ripening. Sadly yesterday disaster struck in the way of a massive storm of rain and huge hailstones with more promised later this week. This untimely spiteful force not only decimated fruit trees, most of the flowers and parts of our electric equipment but it also revived the tomato blight which as I speak is once again rampaging through the crop at an alarming rate. This time I fear the end is nigh for them. I am reliably informed that it is possible to ripen tomatoes in a draw along with a banana, so I intend to give this a go with some of them. The remainder are heading towards a large vat of (Val Frazier's recipe) green tomato chutney, which will then be distributed as Xmas presents to all the family along with a bottle of my recently prepared courgette wine!

Last month we had to visit UK twice, once for a funeral and once for a wedding. For the former we were near the south coast so decided to take in the weekend in Dartmouth, with its quirky little streets and tucked away pubs. Sadly it rained torrentially all weekend but in the main it was still enjoyable once we had managed to find and pay a fortune for a parking space. On our first night we decided to spoil ourselves and visit a restaurant that boasted a Michelin star which was run by some double-barrel named TV chef. He was not in residence of course as he was away in London lining his pockets making some program about food from South West from which he undoubtedly will cash in yet another cookbook in time for Xmas. Instead we were left in the capable hands of his phoney accented French matre'd who went by the name of "Fabreeze", (something which made us giggle as to us this is the name of a cleaning product). I suspect he was actually from Walsall, real name Barry! I have to admit the food was excellent but the service I felt was below par. For instance, as we live near one of the worlds wine capitals, I have developed a perfectly capable skill of pouring my own wine and thus take offence to a waiter refuelling my glass after every sip. Indeed if he did that at our home the poor guy would be physically worn-out. Eventually I felt the need to tell him this, but as the restaurant was only half full all his other colleagues seized the opportunity to do his job for him, with the ultimate aim of emptying our bottle and offering us another. As you can imagine the cost per bottle would keep us in wine for a month where we live so I was unimpressed by the large Glaswegian waitress with her rather interesting tattoos and her coarse sales banter of "…how this particular vintage was singled out by her boss from some hidden away vineyard etc...". We didn't leave a tip.

On our second night I spent twenty quid on local ingredients (and an acceptable Chilean Chardonnay) to prepare us a nice 2 course fish dinner on our balcony overlooking the Dart, wondering how one qualified to get one of those coveted Michelin stars and whether perhaps I should submit an application.

Our other trip was altogether more enjoyable in the fabulous city of Edinburgh. Although it is Wendy's home town and somewhere I have visited regularly for work, neither of us have taken the time to be there as tourists. Not the "traipsing down the Royal Mile and buying *Jimmy* hats" sort of tourists, but the more subtle kind enjoying some of the more understated parts that the capital has to offer. Firstly we visited the vast Portobello beach which was totally deserted except for a few folks walking their dogs, despite it being a nice day by Scotland's standards. It did, however, make me miss our own dogs who would have had endless fun chasing the seagulls and splashing in the shallows. In France dogs are not allowed on the beach, a rule which possibly has been specifically instigated to prevent the behaviour of our two. For example, Cassis (her with the almost recovered haircut) has a very friendly habit of pouncing on small children and sharing their ice creams, something which tends to alarm their parents somewhat. Louis on the other hand has an incredible capacity to cock his leg on anything and everything, including unsuspecting sunbathers, which doesn't go down too well either. Also, due to his spaniel ancestry he enjoys digging holes and has a well honed ability to launch projectile sand up to a credible 20 feet or so, often directly over the same tourists he has visited earlier. All in all, the busy sands of Southern France are a rather embarrassing place to take them and something we would have to avoid even if we were allowed.

We then visited Edinburgh's beautiful Royal Botanical gardens and marvelled at all the plants growing in controlled environments under glass, many of which adorned our own garden back home in Aquitaine. Armed with my trusty scissors I did borrow a few cuttings though, probably getting caught on camera in the process, which I will cultivate in "Dr Potty's potting shed" as Wendy has named it.

But my most enjoyable visit was to a second hand book shop, run by a fascinating bespectacled bearded 82 year old gentleman, tucked away in a side street near Leith. I would imagine it got a few visitors per week at most but it hosted some absolute gems and specialised in Scottish heritage. I was particularly taken with a large leather bound ledger called the "Complete Farmer" which was an encyclopedia of all things agricultural pre 1820, but sadly as it was priced at £350 I could only flick through it in the shop rather than study it in the comfort of my own time. The old boy was probably worth millions and

I am sure he could afford to replace his well-worn slippers if he so wished, but I don't think I have ever seen anyone more happy in their work.

Where we live is reasonably central between Bordeaux and Bergerac airports, both of whom run services of "budget" airlines to UK. For those unfamiliar with these, for a smaller than usual fee travellers are herded like sheep on and off an aircraft and glared and barked at by some unbelievably rude staff whilst being sold outrageously priced drinks and snacks, most of which are inedible. As I spend much of my time wearing plastic sandals, I usually discard them as soon as I get on board. However, I have twice recently be commanded to "put my shoes on for landing", so the last time I questioned on what grounds this was necessary? For instance was I required to walk away from an air-crash and thus my feet needed protection from fire? Or perhaps I would be called upon to take control of the cockpit in an emergency landing and hence would hurriedly require my sandals to in order to use the pedals? Maybe it was my sarcasm that sparked the ensuing attitude of "Brunhilde of the skies", or possibly it was my questioning if she had been a "milk monitor" in her school days. Either way I was informed in no uncertain terms that if I did not comply I may be arrested and thrown in a Turkish prison or possibly nailed to a wooden cross in Stansted airport as a testament to this ogre's supreme power. As I still got no acceptable explanation for this ridiculous ruling I decided check it out on Google. It transpires that in the event of a crash landing my sandals may be hurled about the cabin doing unspeakable damage to other passengers, possibly decapitating the pilot and all his crew in the process. Pretty obvious really, I should have realised that M&S flip-flops are indeed lethal weapons, despite them not bearing a government health warning! Last week I travelled with a different airline called *jet2.com* who not only had no such ruling but were positively polite and charming. This leads me to ponder the question whether good manners are only available at a higher price rather than as our constitutional rights?

Parrots and preserves

August 2009

This year has seen a record crop of fruit in this area, with trees bowing and straining under the weight. So the time of year has come to let the imagination run wild in the chutney department. Having started early making my green tomato chutney, we moved on to apricot & green bean pickle, 2 different apricot jams, peach/apple & lemon relish, plumb & chilli sauce (specifically for marinating duck breasts), and my most recent butternut squash/aubergine & sour-grape hot pickle . We also have sun dried tomatoes and pickled walnuts. I tend to be a shoot-from-the-hip cook, and rarely use a recipe or even write anything down, despite being regularly asked by friends. We also end up with far too much produce as it is impossible to eat it all in a year and the empty jars are too costly to give away to anyone whom may not return them. So this year I have had a brainwave. In late September, we are to host the 1st (and possibly last) annual Aquitaine Chutney festival. It will be a meeting of chutney-heads, with opportunity to discuss and swap recipes, as well as competing classes for chutneys, pickles, jams etc. Entries are welcome from anywhere, and prizes will be awarded by our invited chutney specialist judge (still looking for a volunteer on that one). We will also be offering produce for sale and this is where I can hopefully unload some of my 2008 vintage courgette chutney. Method in the madness!

I often use the word peasant to describe the rural local French people, not as a derogatory term, but because it is a general British expression that has come down through the ages. Rural France is probably 30 years behind its cosmopolitan comparison in Britain and, as was in UK in the 70's, there is a huge gulf between the chic and somewhat worldly city dwellers of Paris and Bordeaux to the locals here in the south west, who still have morals, (if the French ever had morals) and earn a living from the land. Growing up on the family farm in Rock, as a teenager I was constantly reminded that "you never saw a farmer on a bike" and various other delusional statements from locals who perceived farmers as some kind of land barons hoarding cash under their beds. For me to evolve into a city worker, wearing a suit, and eventually living in a busy city centre could never have been conceived at that age, but that is by the by. Of course nowadays a large percentage of UK's rural communities are populated by folks who earn their livings in the city, and country and townsfolk mainly live side by side in relative harmony.

The local peasant farmer here in South West France is not unlike that one of rural England in the 70's, except a he drives a white van instead of a land-rover (or a bike). He generally maintains a low profile, and declares his poverty to all, apart from when he exercises his shiny new EEC funded monster tractors in the nearby fields. From time to time he does act a little strange though. For instance, when did you ever go into a restaurant, and the peasant family on the next table have their pet parrot with them? I kid you not, the table set for 4 contained 3 peasants as follows:

Father peasant, complete with rugged complexion, worried eyes, threadbare jumper, scrubbed hands.

Mother peasant, bad hair, quilted overcoat (in June), calculating expression, tightly gripped purse.

Daughter peasant, 13 going on 50, thick rimmed glasses, risqué gold stud earrings, bored gaze.

And then this damn parrot, all yellow and red feathers. It had a place set for it, and was happily consuming French onion soup. The family were all sitting there, and not a word was uttered from any of them, not even the bird. Come to think of it, it was the best behaved bird I have ever witnessed anywhere, let alone in a fine eatery such as this.

They quietly ate their 4 course meal, all 4 of them, and then left in a small white van, presumably back to their peasant dwelling. I will admit, I scratched my head in astonishment, but everyone seemed oblivious to this odd behaviour which is possibly normal among peasants. It was all a bit surreal.

When growing up, like most boys I was always fascinated by gadgets and even now I take a passing interest at what is on the market, although in French shops this is often last years equipment. However Wendy, my better half, seems to have an assortment of gadgets that are so overly complicated that a degree in science is required to use them. OK, so she does have a degree in science, but even so, why so many settings? Last winter her hairdryer was required to thaw out frozen pipes while she was away in UK. After 20 minutes of shivering in the attic I eventually had to phone her just to find out how to switch the blasted thing on. An array of colour coded switches confronted me, none of which seemed to do anything. Apparently these were "settings", and the ON switch was operated by pressing and holding a few of these in sequence. How was I to know that? Would it be too difficult for the manufacturers to give me a hint? It's the same with the TV. We have a sack full of remote controls which tune us in to various channels, satellites, DVD players etc. But the hardest part is actually switching on the TV itself. Again this is achieved by pressing and holding one red button, then the yellow one followed by the green one, I think. I have suggested to her that maybe she should just buy appliances with a simple on/off button, but her wily retort was "…shame I wasn't fitted with one"!

Whilst sitting enjoying breakfast on the terrace one morning recently a couple of scruffy looking chaps appeared on the steps wearing jeans and baseball caps. I confess I was somewhat startled and considered the possibility that they may be burglars or perhaps deranged psychopaths on the run. However, when assessing the danger of the situation I noted they carried clipboards which didn't actually look too physically threatening. On closer inspection I noted said clipboards contained plans of our house, and after some deliberation I established these two thugs were actually from the planning office. Somewhat different from British civil servants I have encountered, but none the less all powerful and inquisitive. Well we have a large tobacco barn joined on to the north west of the house which is 100 square metres or so, and probably 10 metres high. We have got ideas of one day developing it into a separate dwelling or maybe an extension to our house, so over the last year I have laid foundations and we have got as far as concreting the floor complete with under floor waste pipes. It appeared that it was this that our visitors were keen to investigate, and they immediately started measuring things and taking notes in what appeared to be a disapproving tone. I have no idea why they were here without an appointment but it is my opinion that our local Marie may have a good set of "regulation issue" binoculars, and could just have spotted my active concrete mixer recently. He must have considered "aha, more bureaucracy, more taxes, ooh-la-la" and consequently sent his henchmen round for a nose. For those unaware, the Marie is a very powerful person in France, elected democratically, supposedly. I have read some of the columns in this paper about the administrations and council issues in Rock, and realise they are very far removed from what we have in this once socialist country. We have actually met our Marie, whom we visited empty handed one day to enquire about a few local issues. He was all smiles and admitted that his grandfather once lived in our house, but he did look gravely disappointed that we hadn't arrived at his palatial office with a bottle of something drinkable and preferably vintage! And Britain thinks it has political problems? I am pretty sure this gangster's expense sheet might make good reading in the Telegraph. For the record, we do have every intention of putting in an application for development but only if and when we could afford to undertake the structural work, but we are also aware that the decision rides primarily with one man. I will say no more in case he gets a monthly subscription to the R&DN!

Visitors and magpies

September 2009

Wow, what a summer we have had here in South West France. I think we had one days rain in August which for some reason coincided with the only day I played golf. C'est la vie! The nice weather has brought us a steady stream of visits by friends and family over the past 6 weeks, one of the perils and delights of living in a warmer climate. Some have overlapped causing us to utilise all our attic rooms, but occasionally we have managed a few days between visits to "freshen up". The dogs have had a ball, finding new sleeping partners and favourite dinner guests amongst the youngsters. Louis has only managed to cock his leg on one guest, which is almost commendable given his affliction in such matters. Our vegetable garden has been somewhat depleted, and I am sure many of our guests will never want to see a French bean again. Most departed with at least one jar of tomato chutney.

This year we seemed to be plagued with magpies or "les pie" as they are called in French. I know the old rhyme "1 for sorrow, 2 for joy etc", but am not sure what we get for 14? *14 for a peach crop, totally destroyed?* Perhaps the editor of this publication could hold a competition to populate this rhyme up to 20 for me? (Maybe my Mother should enter since she is such a genius with her limericks!). Wendy is not too keen on having a gun in the house otherwise I would take the matter into my own hands. Time to construct some sort of humane trap methinks.

Whilst on that subject, shortly begins the *Chasse* season in France. This is when licensed hunters roam the countryside in brightly coloured jackets, shooting at anything that moves, including small birds, rodents, deer and wild boar. Literally everything in sight. As we only have 9 acres of ground we have the opportunity to decline them access to our land by means of signs displaying the words "reserve de chasse". I think the law here entitles "right to roam" (and shoot) on land plots of 20 acres and upwards. Most of them heed these signs although evidently their dogs cannot read them. Many a morning we see a couple of hounds burling past our back door in hot pursuit of one of our cats, which intelligently scarper up trees out of reach. Our dogs usually join the melee in a combination of barking and bottom sniffing before the animals are recalled by their masters. Pooper then spends the next 12 hours barking in case they return. It's all quite irritating. It is my guess that "les pie" are also aware of these signs and hence their residence "*chez nous*". Incidentally, I have recently been informed (yes, by that bloke I met in the pub) that the reason they wear such brightly coloured jackets is so they can be spotted by other hunters and avoid being shot by the aimless gunfire around the hedgerows! Evidently, wild animals are colour-blind?

As the summer starts to fade, so starts the rugby season. I have just heard that our local team (Marmande) has this year been bolstered by the addition of a young player from Tenbury Wells by the name of Alex James, whose father runs Tenbury Farm supplies. He has been signed on a professional contract so my colleagues and I will become keen supporters this winter to watch his progress at the club. Considering the size of France this is somewhat of a coincidence, especially given that my youngest son actually plays rugby for Tenbury, although the 2 of them didn't know each other.

This time of year also sees wine festival period, so a few weeks ago we visited the Duras event. This is a little known but excellent wine region 40 minutes south of the more prominent Bordeaux area. We were each presented with a wine glass ingeniously suspended by a cord which goes around the neck with which we could then use for free wine tasting from representations from 30 or so vineyards from the region. As I was driving I utilised my option to spit out each mouthful into vessels provided and tasted probably 50 or so wines, being particularly taken by a medal winning 2005 Cabernet/Merlot made by an English company called Chater. Well worth looking for on UK shelves I would say, although may be a little pricey. The rest of my passengers took the more conventional approach of drinking anything and everything on offer, and the suspended wine glass became something of a necessity towards end of the afternoon. As I poured them into the car it was evident that maybe some of the other visitors were perhaps prone to sampling a few and then chancing their arm behind the wheel. I counted no less than 40 police holding roadblocks and making random breath tests. Quite right too. The afternoon did allow me to add a few nice bottles to my slowly expanding wine cave. For those unaware, 2005 was one of the best wine years in France for a long time. As James May would say, *this is a wine fact.* 2009 may possibly be a good one too, but we need to wait and see how the September mists affect the crop at harvest time. As we speak, I am shining up my own demi-johns ready to embark on producing "Chateaux Chauffour", a cheeky little number made from our 2 white sauvignon vines in the garden. It is highly unlikely it will reach the shelves of Oddbins. Some may recall a few months ago I made some courgette wine, which has now since stopped fermenting but I haven't been brave enough to taste it yet as it has gone a rather peculiar colour. No prizes for guessing what the family are getting for Xmas.

We have recently been to a French wedding which featured heavily with ex-Rockers, the bride having been born on the Greenway in a house my family once owned. Her family, who have lived in Aquitaine for 12 years now, are close friends of ours and one of the reasons we too moved to this area. Many of the wedding guests were also friends who do live or have once lived in the Rock parish and it was great to all catch up again, some of whom I hadn't seen in 10 years. We wish India Prince and her new husband Gerald all the very best. Whilst on the subject of coincidences, Gerald was born in the tiny town of Pont-du-Casse which is twinned with none other than that "Town in the Orchard", Tenbury Wells. Small world, eh?

That takes this year's social event count to 3 weddings and a funeral. As this seemed an untidy figure I recently asked my *"old hen"* to be my wife, just to round up the numbers, as it were. She dutifully accepted although we may not actually go through with the deed until next year now.

Hippies and the M25.

October 2009

Once again we have had a few visitors this month, including once Rock local who may remain nameless. This fit chap went for a run in the wooded countryside, only to forget the way back home again and a half hour jog ended up as a 90 minutes endurance test! May I recommend a personal gps system or at the very least a trail of bread crumbs be used on future occasions? At least he shouldn't get lost trekking the 10 yards or so home from the Rock Cross of a Friday night!

I have always understood the term "tree-huggers" as a derogatory phrase for people who over enthusiastically enjoy plants and wildlife, and who possibly get hyper-sensitive when trees are being chopped or removed for no good reason. But I am now enlightened that the term has real substance. Across the field from us we have a huge and beautiful old oak tree, next to a windmill. It is one of those perfect ones that a child would draw, totally symmetrical and spreading its braches on the horizon. One day last week a young female arrived near the tree complete with her rucksack, as we serenely gazed out over another fabulous sunny autumn evening. But then having put down her spoils, she did a little exercise somewhere between line-dance and morris-dance around the old tree. After this had finished, she then proceeded to throw her arms around the tree and lovingly hugged it for a good 10 minutes or so. As the trunk is in excess of a metre thick, she was unable to reach around the whole girth, so she repeated this a few times until it was well and truly hugged. I am at pains to point out that unfortunately at no time during this exercise did she remove all her clothes, possibly as she had seen the glint of sun reflected off my field-glasses or maybe she was just a little conservative on this issue. Whatever, she then sauntered off, potentially on a quest to hug every other nice tree in the area. I resisted the temptation to start my chainsaw at this point! I have no idea why she chose this particular tree, or this area or even this country, but maybe somewhere out there, there is a "Rough guide to huggable trees", from which she selected it? Or possibly she was on a world tour of compassionate hardwoods? I will do some research on the subject, and maybe even contact the tree-hugging organisation, suggesting that they would get much closer to the trees if they did it in fact do it naked, obviously enforcing an acceptable age restriction beforehand!

While on the subject of hippies, I was in UK recently and picked up a copy of a weekend broadsheet newspaper. Although we sometimes buy this paper in France, the UK version includes many more supplements to the point where it is so heavy one requires a back-truss to carry it home, an exercise that would be nigh on impossible on my Sunday morning cycle ride to the "shop". In the gardening supplement I read an article by a "Jenny Bloom" who runs a landscape gardening business, and who was advising readers on how to get back to nature. I was astounded to discover that for many of her clients she was planting hawthorn, blackthorn and brambles. By contrast, these are very plants that I have spent the last 2 years trying hard to remove from our own garden with finger piercing result. She also advised people not to mow their lawns, instead leaving them 2 feet high to allow wild flowers (weeds) to establish themselves. So there we go, I have been doing it all wrong? Basically, I should just leave it all alone to get along by its self. And to think I could have paid her for that advice. I also note that her partners, Todd Longstaffe-Wagstaffe and Felix Double-Barrelled, have recently helped her create an overgrown wilderness, known as the "healing garden", for the Prince Charles Trust. It went on to win a gold medal at the Chelsea flower show no less. Does anyone else see a similarity to the emperor's new clothes here? Surely this surpasses even Damien Hurst's ridiculous offerings as con of the century? She finally added "..when society breaks down, I will live off my hedgerows…"! Excuse me? Presumably you will thrive on rose-hips, black-berries, mayflies and possibly magic mushrooms? Judging by her inset photo she has perhaps been dragged backwards through one already. I couldn't help wondering what colour the sky must be on her planet? Or furthermore how the editor of what was once termed as an intellectual newspaper can be blinded into publishing such delusional rubbish?

For a short while this month we have had to spend some time in UK for family reasons. I made the trip compete with dogs over the channel and up to Teesside by car in one go, taking a period of 20+ hours. En-route I was delayed at Calais by the British customs who spotted that the dogs' passports had been signed by our vet at 3.30pm the previous day, and the fact that it was now only 1.30pm they would have to wait for 2 hours until an exact period of 24 hours had passed before they could enter British waters. It was at this point that I realised I was returning to "jobsworth land", a nation of civil servants and political correctness, and after a role of the eyes I seriously considered turning tail for home while my temper was still intact. However, I stayed on track and whiled away 2 hours at the port until we were allowed to board the ferry pondering the insane officialdom that has recently engulfed these British islands. Shortly afterwards I came to a bridge over the river Thames at Dartford. A fee of £1.50 was required to cross it and it was then that I realised that I had absolutely no English money with me, only euro's in coins. I offered the Mr Civil Servant five euro coins in exchange for £1.50, a fair exchange I reckon, but it was more than his "job's worth" and I then felt the wrath of the local police and their very impressive guns. I was directed out of the queue, across 17 lanes of traffic which had been stopped specifically for my purpose by my extremely important gun-slinging escort, and sent packing to find a cash point. I was told in no uncertain terms not to darken their door again until I returned with proper money. The sniggering could be heard from the queues far and wide, as "Mr

Frenchie" was put in his place, our car having French number plates. It took me an hour to find a cash point, and once more I considered heading back to France the way I had come.

I eventually arrived in Billingham, a small town near Middlesbrough, where Wendy's mother lives. The town bears many similarities to west midland towns, being born out of the 1960's boom in the chemical business, and the huge growth of ICI who at one stage employed 20,000 people in this area. Since the decline of this industry, the town is now struggling and crying out for regeneration in much the same way that Kidderminster has had to cope with the loss of the carpet trade. A small suburban semi-detached may now be my home for a few weeks, at least until we get things sorted out. For many this would be a welcome return to civilisation, with its convenience stores, central heating, sliced bread, take-away curries and Tetley bitter, compared to the very rural existence we normally tolerate in France. But for me, although I will try and make the best of it, I will struggle to settle without my picturesque views and the open space of our French farmhouse. I had just about mastered conversational French and here I am now having to decipher Geordie! The dogs are enjoying themselves though, with walks in the park and new places and smells, although they are quite disturbed that people with dogs should be allowed to walk past the front window. We have already had an eventful trip to the beach where they barked at other dogs in their French accents, chased seagulls into the sea, and then one of them ran away. Despite my shouting he failed return for 20 minutes, dicing with a main road in the process. I'm not sure where he thought he was off too, France I suppose. I guess the dogs were finding it hard to be understood too although I fail to see how that effected his hearing!

On the subject of seaside, a few weeks ago we took them to the Atlantic coast for the day, and they spent many hours frolicking around in the water on a nicely deserted beach near Bordeaux. The next day Louis, our pointer, had his tail between his legs and was generally being miserable. We left it for a day or so before considering approaching the vet, when we then discovered on Google that he was suffering from a condition known as "limp tailed syndrome". My suggestion of a cure by Viagra was met with considerable distaste by my fiancé! It appeared that the problem would rectify itself within a few days, which it did. The condition, apparently quite common in pointers and other hunting dogs, is something to do with the fact that Louis wags his tail constantly and the prolonged immersion in cold water affected this. So basically that is his penance for being too happy. Rough justice I say. It's a bit like your face hurting when you smile. Come to think of it, maybe this is a condition that affects civil servants, particularly those operating the toll booths on the M25?

Fall time

November 2009

Earlier on in the month I visited my parents in Rock for the first time in 7 months. We descended en-mass complete with dogs who were elated to get a run around the farm and surrounding fields. Not sure that my mothers aged dog was quite so pleased to see them though as they do bounce about a bit. It was good to catch up with auld acquaintances and even get a beer in the local pub from the editor. We also witnessed AJ, the youngest member of the Neath clan getting his first slurp of Guinness before he reaches 1 year old! I am sure his great grandfather and namesake would have been proud. In the pub I bumped into another "local" who expressed his desire to visit us in France based on what he had read in this column. Unfortunately it wont be for a few more months yet, until the glue is dry on the aeroplane he is building to make the trip with. John, I will ensure the grass is well mown on the landing strip and fit for purpose come spring. Just try not to fly too close to the sun!

Whilst there, my mother introduced me to a wonderful French opera that she has recently taken to, called "La Juive" (the jewess). A highly powerful tale of a love affair between a Jewish goldsmith's daughter and a Christian prince, who is played very ably by the great Neil Shikoff. This opera was one of the most controversial works of the 19th century due to its tricky subject matter, and is believed to have subsequently influenced the status of jews in French society. It seemed quite surreal to discover this whilst on English soil and I am now hunting down a copy of it over here.

This month has been a bit of an awkward one for us, with Wendy and the dogs in UK and me home here in France for most of the month like "billy no-mates". But I will admit during this time I have had a small wave of international visitors to keep me company. Four welsh ones turned up quite unexpectedly and brought some miserable weather with them. As they could see I had been struggling to maintain the housework due to circumstances of excess travel and work, they did roll up their sleeves though, and whilst I was out they cleaned the house, removed cobwebs and even fired up the Ford tractor to mow the grass. I was thankful for that. Probably not the relaxing time they had envisaged though and they were surely glad to go home for rest. They were then succeeded by a couple of kiwi's whom I had met in New Zealand five years ago. Again, as well as being thankful for the company it was nice to come in from work in the evening to find the fire lit and some tea on the hob. They also helped me make some chutney from our Persimmon fruit (I think known as Sharron fruit in UK?), which was surprisingly nice considering how horrendously bitter the unripe fruit can be. As they had come from the fabulous Marlborough wine making region of NZ, I felt obliged to take them to visit some of our better vineyards. We made a sortie to St Emillion where the name alone commands a premium of upwards of £10 per bottle and we saw bottles for sale of £500+. Who on earth would pay that much? And why? It was worth sampling a few though, it would be rude not to really! On returning to our house I felt the urge to uncork one of my recently made "Chateau Chauffour" 2009 whites. Surprisingly they liked it, although I am not sure I do. It can at the very least be described as "interesting"! It may have matured to a good vintage by the time we do the re-match in Auckland in 2011, hopefully celebrating us winning the rugby world cup final, eh girls!

This time of year is *Chasse* season in France. This is when licensed hunters roam the countryside in brightly coloured jackets, shooting at anything that moves, including small birds, rodents, deer and wild boar. Literally everything in sight. As we only have 9 acres of ground we have the opportunity to decline them access to our land by means of signs displaying the words "reserve de chasse". I think the law here entitles "right to roam" (and shoot) on land plots of 20 acres and upwards. Most of them heed these signs although evidently their dogs cannot read them. Many a morning we see a couple of hounds burling past our back door in hot pursuit of one of our cats, which intelligently scarper up trees out of reach. Our dogs usually join the melee in a combination of barking and bottom sniffing before the animals are recalled by their masters. Pooper then spends the next 12 hours barking in case they return. It's all quite irritating. 2 cats have gone missing recently but I am sure this may be a coincidence. Incidentally, I have recently been informed (yes, by that bloke I met in the pub) that the reason they wear such brightly coloured jackets is so they can be spotted by other hunters and avoid being shot by the aimless gunfire around the hedgerows! Evidently, wild animals are colour-blind?

Last month I once again got caught out by the clocks altering due to the wretched daylight saving time, getting up an hour too early and generally feeling foolish. I have never truly grasped the concept of this. I once read an interview with a wise old Indian from Arizona, who when questioned why they didn't not observe daylight saving time in that state replied, "only a government could believe that you could cut a foot off the top of a blanket, sew it on the bottom and have a longer blanket". I couldn't agree more!

One doesn't like to stereotype people to their locations especially in these days of a multi cultural society, although I think we all secretly like to believe that traditions are universally upheld wherever possible. During my stay in England's North East this month I looked out from the window of our adopted semi-detached to witness a small fury animal moving across the football pitch on a Saturday afternoon at an alarming rate. Whilst pondering this spectacle I noted the obviously artificial creature was then being chased by some equally supersonic dogs. Yes, I was witnessing whippet racing, the north east's equivalent of Morris dancing and the stuff of legends. I have never seen so many cloth caps outside of a period TV drama. I was overawed with emotion, and inspired to consider what other sporting traditions may well still be being pursued in various parochial corners of that country. On investigation it appears that cheese rolling, Closh and Shove-piggy-shove all have represented societies somewhere in UK and are still being practiced with staunch enthusiasm. Not sure if burning witches is still allowed in UK anymore though although it may possibly still be legal in France? I must check. I am quite sure I could compile a waiting list if it were.

The Frozen North

December 2009

Another whirlwind winter month has seen me spend more time in UK than in France. Sadly last month we have had bereavement in the family with the passing of David George, my brother-in-law. Dave has been a regular visitor to our house in France and always offered a great contribution to the festivities. It has been a sad time, but my sister and her family have been extremely strong. We wish them all our heartfelt best wishes.

I have spent much of the last month clearing out the attic in Wendy's mothers house in Teeside, cataloguing things and checking out prices and loading stuff on EBAY. It is so surprising what is valuable. A beautifully engraved 1930's sewing machine which would make a lovely ornament in any home is worth £10 at most. Yet a 1968 plastic Barbie doll is upwards of £50 with extra for clothes and accessories, some Ladybird and Enid Blyton books worth £10 apiece and even a fake 1970's fur coat worth £50. It seems it is often down to how rare things are, but I cannot understand who collects all this stuff? Some of the old board games such as Cluedo and Buccaneer are worth 10 times their original cost to people who will never get any fun out of them as we did as kids. Remember Spirograph? Who would be disciplined enough to have one still complete in its box with its original biros? Well Wendy would actually, bless her. Ker-ching ££!

Sports fans among you, you may have noticed many sportsmen displaying rather suspicious moustaches during November, particularly those from down under. It was quite unnerving to see burly Aussie and Kiwi rugby players bearing "spiv-like" facial hair whilst simultaneously rubbing all our home teams into the dirt this autumn. The reason for this bum-fluff approach is due to something known universally as "grow a mo" for November, or "**Movember**" as it is more affectingly termed, and is to raise money and awareness to male health problems such as prostrate cancer. I am not too sure if this concept has been highlighted in UK this year, but one hopes that by next year many British chaps may join in the moustache parade to support such a cause. I already note the united participation of most civil servants in this, but then perhaps facial hair is a pre-requisite of their job? France, of course, are world champions when it comes to the old top-lip accessories, especially the men! The walrus-of-the-year award surely has to go to the nice policeman who recently nicked me for not wearing a seatbelt whilst driving less than 100 yards around the village square a few months ago. The 90 euro on-the-spot fine (in cash) that I was forced to part with has hopefully gone towards his investment in some grooming equipment so that he can at least eat his frogs legs without having to filter it through his "yard-brush" moustache first!

On the subject of good causes, I recently received a circular email containing a very moving true story about some of our soldiers transferring through Heathrow airport amidst rapturous public applause. I won't retell the tail in full, but it involved a 6 year old girl whose father was on active service in Afghanistan and she asked them to check if he was ok. The mail was sent to me by a good friend whose son is also over there at present, and she is obviously worried about his safety. The upshot of the email was to announce something called RED FRIDAYS, which involves anyone who cares being urged to wear something red **every** Friday as a mark of support for our troops. I am not sure how far this issue has been publicised in Britain, but I for one see no harm in extending our annual poppy day to a weekly quieter appreciation of the same appeal if it can make a difference. Ok maybe not the Santa outfit all year round, but perhaps some red fliplops at the very least.

In the run up to Xmas, I saw on TV that much of the countries supply of mistletoe still hails from the Teme Valley, with local councillor Reg Farmer pictured gathering his annual harvest. This is something we rarely see in France, despite our living in a fruit growing area. Perhaps it is because the French don't require an annual excuse to kiss each other as this is something they do so frequently anyway, who knows. But the great thing about Xmas in France is that it still maintains its traditional concept. Yes there are sometimes tacky Xmas decorations on a few houses, specifically with the model of Santa climbing up the balcony. But generally Xmas is not hijacked by commercialism in the same way it is in UK. There is a refreshing lack of imported turkey and crackers and kids only expect one modest present each, possibly made of wood. No it's not quite still Dickensian but it is certainly a distant reminder of how things were when we were growing up compared with the greedy Britain of today. Only with more cheese, obviously.

Having had to make the regular journey between the midlands and the north east a few times recently, can anybody explain to me the reason for the continual 50 mph speed restrictions on the M1 and M42? For stretches of 20 miles at a time, the cameras are set to monitor average speeds that exceed this. In most cases this is during 3 clear lanes, with no indication of any road works in progress, and often my journeys have been in the middle of the night when all the workers would be safely tucked up in bed. At least the French have the decency to work through the night to avoid the delays on their main routes. Surely this is some kind of Gordon Brown money making scam? I am hopeful that these cameras can not decipher our French number plates, otherwise I may be returning home to a pile of photos on the doormat in France. My only saviour may be that they cannot possibly see exactly who was driving, in the dark? My time to grow a walrus-like disguise methinks!

Whilst in the Black Country recently I passed a children's nursery called **CARE4URKIDZ**. A few things instantly struck me about this anomaly.

1. Isn't it appalling how mobile phone texting language has no spilled over into the "real" world? Something I still haven't got the hang of.

2. What chance has any child got of learning English when the name of their first school is spelled in such a bewildering way?

3. Surely it is hard enough to understand people from the Dudley in the first place?

4. When a child arrives at school and the teacher says "Yow'm oor rite ar kid?", how would they write this down in their daybook? I dread to think!

Perhaps a phrasebook to cover this translation problem might be a bestseller? What a bostin idea!

By the time this goes to print, all that is left of Xmas will be pine needles and credit card bills. Happy New Year everyone or Bon Annee, as we say in these parts.

And   finally,   to   quote   from   my   new phrasebook......**Tararabit**...

Rambling

January 2010

At last, after a prolonged period in UK we have arrived back in France, to better weather, an overgrown garden, decent food, some thin cats and slightly less madness….our new years eve in the north east England a distant memory. One that was highlighted by a local delicacy at Hornsey's Bar and Grill in Seaton Carew in the shape of a pie & pea supper. To be precise, *chef's mince pie served with homemade chips, mushy peas, gravy and…champagne!* Have I missed France? U-betcha.

Trying to make the most of our UK stay, we took a few days off last month in a cottage near Bamburgh in Northumberland. The place was in the middle of a field overlooking Budle bay with lovely sea views from the windows. It was gorgeous, tranquil, remote, and much deserved after the trauma of 2 family funerals in as many months. It was also, however, on a national footpath. As the path ran alongside our conservatory our dogs were once again at a loss as to why people dared to trail past our door at all hours so they barked furiously at them. One thing we don't get in France are ramblers. As the French enjoy the "right to roam", walkers, tourists and locals wander about where ever they want, and generally avoid disturbing residents if they can. They understand livestock and walk around crops rather than through them. They also dress sensibly.

So what is it with this ridiculous dress code that the Ramblers in UK seem to adhere to?

i) Brightly coloured jackets are handy in the wilderness, or even the Sahara. But surely anyone wanting to see wildlife, or at least get close to nature would wear green and brown, not primary colours of red, yellow and blue?

ii) Ski poles? Why? Yes, useful when negotiating the north face of K2, but are they really required for walking along a footpath? A nut stick cut from the hedgerow will suffice if conditions are slippery, and is so much cheaper. And it is eco-mentally friendly.

iii) And what could someone possibly need to carry on a 2 hour walk that requires the use of a rucksack? A brightly coloured one at that. When I go walking I take a bottle of water in my pocket. I eat before I leave the car, or in the pub, or when I get back, with the possible exception of a mars bar which I have a special pocket for. I have a rough idea of the weather forecast so I don't need 2 changes of clothes let alone my entire wardrobe. My map goes in another pocket, so does my compass, torch and a whistle for attracting attention. I also keep a couple of pockets spare, to warm my hands in.

iv) The other day I saw a man wearing two Tesco bags on his feet. What's that about? I felt pained to point out to him that whilst he was in Tescos getting the bags he could just as easily have purchased a perfectly acceptable pair of wellingtons for £6.99.

I have a theory that Ramblers wear all this obtuse stuff so that other people know that they actually are RAMBLERS....important people, making sure the countryside is being maintained, as they trample through it in their droves. My theory concludes that this gear is in fact, a **uniform**. One not dissimilar to that of a traffic warden, only more colourful!

While in Rock for a week or so at Christmas, we went for a walk down through the Whytehouse farm with our dogs, in the snow. When we reached the brook at Woresley I was amazed to find not one or even two, but ten or more brand new wooden bridges at 200 yard intervals spanning the stream that borders the farm with the neighbours. As a child I used to play, swim and even fish in that stream and I have to admit that it is a beautiful spot. I think it is great that others are now encouraged to share the undisputed beauty of these places but surely if someone heads out to enjoy the countryside they are expected to have some degree of mobility and enough intelligence to negotiate the basic obstacles? I am delighted to say that I managed to cross the stream, in full flow, in my wellies without catastrophe and without the aid of a special expensive ski pole. But thank you to the council anyway, for spending tens of thousands of tax payers money on building the bridges, because Wendy & I enjoyed playing Pooh-sticks on one of them. For those of you unable to remember this game, ask someone older. And while you are at it, ask them how in years gone by they managed to cross Dick Brook without the aid of an industrially constructed bridge? They probably didn't have council tax in those days either.

During the weeks we spent clearing out the house in Teesside I had to make numerous journeys with car loads of rubbish to the tip. Except that it is no longer called a 'tip', but is now called the 'Civic Amenities Centre'. Yes, another example of deranged civil servants dreaming up eco friendly and confusing names for all things traditional. Anyway, nowadays at the CAC one has to separate household waste into so many different categories it is utterly confusing as to what goes where. Fortunately there is an army of mysterious little men in a hut who lie in wait, not to advise you, but to shout at you if you dare put a plastic mop in the 'plastics' bin or a wooden toy in the 'wooden materials' bin. I counted 5 of them in all. "Not in there" one yells in his broad Geordie dictatorial brogue "a mop is household stuff, it goes in the general waste bin, way-eye-man (or equally northern expression)". Obviously I should have read my monthly expensive eco-leaflet (printed on recycled paper) first, so that I could identify the error of my ways. However, I did identify that an old record player was in fact an electrical appliance and smugly went to throw it into the correct bin. But no. "Don't throw it in" he commanded. Seemingly he had to slice off the electrical lead and plug first. For what reason? I didn't dare ask.

On leaving I noticed in my rear view mirror these chaps were sorting through the rubbish and retrieving items that may be of some value, presumably selling them on ebay. In their woolly hats they looked like latter day Wombles. Except of course, the Wombles weren't paid the council.

Whilst on the subject of recycling, we recently had to visit the registrar's office to register the death of Wendy's mother in Middlesbrough. Amongst the rack of leaflets on just about everything you can and cannot do these days, I spotted one on the environmental impact of a funeral, indicating how one can do one's bit for the "green world" by following some guidelines. A document so useful that it is written in 8 languages, including Arabic, Mandarin, Kurdish and Urdu, but surprisingly not in French. It basically told bereaved families how they were destroying the planet by driving to grave sites in their cars and asked them to refrain from sending flowers and possibly using too many tissues (recycled ones only). In and amongst other things in this ludicrous document they were advocating the use of cardboard and wicker coffins, or, and I kid you not, bodies being frozen in liquid nitrogen until brittle then broken up into powder with a hammer. The powder can then be scattered in a place of your choice with absolutely no impact on the ozone layer. What a charming occupation that would be for someone!

So the absurd situation in the UK during the cold weather does not surprise me in the slightest. The fact that the councils have not enough money to supply salt to keep the roads clear is surely inevitable. Not because they have invested all the tax payers' money in some dodgy offshore accounts in the North Atlantic, but because they have squandered their budget on ridiculous bureaucracy under the illusion that they are helping the environment. I suppose the ultimate aim is for everyone to walk on the roads instead of driving, then that would negate the need for salt at all. Except it wouldn't would it? Because then they would need to have more moving walkways, heated pavements and directional signs on every corner in nine languages…including braille.

I deduce from all of this that the world, as we know it, has gone totally bonkers! Will this government be the one that is known for putting the "mental" in environ**mental**ism? You trust these people to run your country? In my opinion, they would struggle to run a warm bath!

Frozen South

February 2010

Winter has certainly taken its toll here in France this year, with some exceptionally hard frosts recorded. Our cold weather comes in off the Atlantic and as we do not benefit from being mollycoddled by the Gulf Stream it generally means business when it arrives. So it was no real surprise when once again all our pipes froze in the attic, leaving us without water for days. Of course when they thawed we had all the usual split pipes and panic. Unfortunately we had more than panic this time as we arrived home after staying over at a friends house to keep warm to find a burst pipe had been running all night and has washed upwards of 5 tons of soil out of the foundations of the house. The kitchen is now teetering on the brink and by the time you read this may well have disappeared down the field towards the abyss. What probably will not have happened by the time you read this is our insurance company doing anything to help, despite them having estimates in triplicate and sending assessors, but not before sending estimates for the assessors who finally assess the estimates. Paper, it seems, is still a vital part of French bureaucracy, in fact this nation alone could contribute more to the end of the world via rain forest desecration than any other. No environment awareness here, not when it comes to form filling. And please no, do not suggest that you send us Gordon once he is out of a job to become our eco-minister, we have already run away from his madness thank you. However, I do thank him for subsidising roof insulation via B&Q in Kidderminster down to a fiver per roll, those 15 rolls came in handy and might just help us avoid the next ice-induced disaster.

Our return to France also saw a reorganisation of our cat population, with only two out of our existing four still in residence. The older of our cats we have had for 3 years, she adopting us as cats do, at the property we lived at before buying this house. We brought her with us when we moved here, doing all the butter on the paws thing which was highly unnecessary as she instantly made herself at home. Shortly after that she gave birth to 6 kittens in the attic, which not only increased our feline population somewhat but also brought multiple colonies of fleas, eventually requiring us to fumigate the house. After that it was not unlike that Nintendo DS brain game trying to keep track of numbers of kittens born versus cats leaving home and our numbers ranged between 2 and 12 over the next few years until it steadied last year. We now have 4 healthy ones all neutered, all thieves, all being fed expensive food regularly and each one having us under its spell. By now the rest have populated all the houses in our neighbourhood and can be periodically spotted sitting in kitchen windows down the lane.

So we were a little surprised that when we returned from a few months absence we find that the older ones have now left, obviously getting their feet under a better and more furtive table. Ah shame, we were down to two…which suited me fine. Except we weren't. Because as two had left so we had gained another one. A smoky grey one, which according to my intended is quite attractive. Well it's evidently attractive to the roaming ginger tom who was also here for a while. So it's back full circle. I have no idea why this creature should wish to take up residence here, the other two cats give it a hard time and the pointer dog spends endless hours barking at it, him being of the belief that if you shout at someone repetitively for long enough they will eventually understand. Come to think of it, that is not unlike the English tourists here trying to communicate with the French locals. The cat just ignores him completely and sits happily by the back door waiting for more kitty-chat. Well it did do until Sunday morning, when it left in a cat basket as fortunately we have just found it a new home, 50 miles away. Why is that cat's seem to like people who don't like cats? They certainly have my measure..

Not being the sort of man who cleans his tools before putting them away, if he puts them away at all that is, this time of year is one of preparation of soon-to-be-required equipment. As always, none of it appears to be in working condition. It seems that the sprayer has taken exception to the frost and is now more of a dribbler, requiring parts for the motor which will be a huge test to both my language and toolbox skills. The lawn mower is cowering in the changing rooms with a note from matron prior to its overload of work when spring arrives. I have to sympathise a wee bit as when the warm rain comes you literally can see the grass growing here, without the aid of those irritating high definition slow motion clips that the BBC insist on showing to persuade overpaid people to subscribe their services. Anyway, the mower is refusing to go on duty and I believe it has put a request in for a transfer to somewhere in the North African desert. The tractor sounds very similar to myself on a cold morning, sort of going through the motions of getting up but not actually opening its eyes. A new battery is required there then, and one for the tractor too. The pool pump, hedge trimmer and chainsaw all require attention, the list is endless and my various methods *percussion* maintenance don't seem to work any more. It is as if there is some sort of solidarity movement going on, one out all out, I blame the French. Or perhaps it's just me being unable to cope with machinery in general, my qualifications of a grade C in O'level woodwork being insufficient for a task of this magnitude. I really should get a proper job. And a gardener.

But the odd sunny days we are getting now indicate that the better weather is just around the corner, the seasons in this part of the world being 4 to 6 weeks earlier than UK. The seedlings are all waiting patiently in their trays in the veranda and a whole array of small plants have emerged from their shells to become fully fledged little shrubs, over 100 in all. It is the first time I have attempted to grow shrubs from seeds but so far have been successful with Oleander, Hibiscus, Lavender and Armante to name but a few. I gathered the seeds from the respective plants last summer and autumn and it is quite satisfying to see them flourish under my care. The plan is to replace all the brambles and rubbish that has taken me two years to clear from around our lake to introduce some colour and beauty to this serene spot. We are not out of the woods yet though (no pun intended) as once they are planted out they will have coypu, red deer, hares and wild boar to contend with. That and the possibility of Louis (the afore mentioned pointer) digging them all out again in one of his frequent deranged sprees of madness. I have also transported Wendy's mothers old garden seat down here from Teesside, complete with its plaque denoting many years of service as a school nanny on her retirement, which will be built in to pride of place amongst flowers overlooking the water. I believe in the past it has witnessed its share of consummation of gin & tonic's and she may rest assured that tradition will be once again upheld with vigour come summer.

Skiing and eggheads
March 2010

It is quite hard to believe that a year has now gone full circle since I started ranting in the monthly publication and here we are once more approaching springtime. I am not sure it is a sign of growing older to admit that time goes by so fast, or just a sign of being too damn busy to notice it as it goes by? I am pained to admit it must be the latter in my case as I seem to spend all of my time rushing around trying to get things done. My current project, operation lake clearance, has worn my limbs down to their sockets as has the physical effort of holding down part-time day job. Somehow or other though, I have miraculously managed to squeeze in writing a novel during this last three months. It is not exactly 'war and peace' but it is a nice little story based on some events in my past and one I wanted to tell. I am not sure where it will go from here; I suspect nowhere, but I enjoyed writing it and guess I will enjoy reading it myself one day which is all that really matters. That is if I ever manage to plough through the backlog of books I have had as presents for the last three Xmases. I think people who know I live in rural boring France buy me huge books on the assumption I have time to spend my life reading them but sadly this is not the case. I wish I did, it would sure as hell beat wielding a scythe and laying concrete blocks.

It is also once again time for rugby international matches and our impending thrashing at the hands of

Les Bleus in Paris. I guess by the time this goes to print that will be done and dusted and I will have eaten a helping of 'gateaux de humble' sprinkled with garlic. We had hoped to visit the game this year, but it appears that the national train service has trebled its prices for that weekend making it cheaper to actually go by taxi for the 6 hour ride than take the fast train. Needless to say, we won't be going. I do love French commerce, it's so predicable.

I have mentioned previously in the column about the quality of French pop music, or lack of it as the case may be. The French all seem to have this rather unhealthy obsession with the singer Johnny Hallyday, France's equivalent of Elvis; an accolade I am sure he would graciously accept. However, he is currently unable to accept anything as he is poorly and has been in a coma, poor chap; but in their attempt to make him better every station has now taken to pouring out his music with unrivalled magnitude. It is becoming unbearable to the point where last week I only just restrained myself from attacking my portable radio with a wood chisel whist at work. I love music of all kinds and at home in winter we opt for playing all sorts of genres rather than watching the rubbish that is on TV most evenings. But I am glad to say we possess no music by this Elvis impersonator whatsoever, a fact in itself that must highlight his ineptitude to entertain me, that and the fact that nobody outside of France has ever heard of him. It would be churlish of me not to wish him a speedy recovery though. On the subject of

evening TV, we somehow or other find ourselves
compelled to watch *Eggheads* most nights, despite us
both finding the 'world greatest quiz team' so
unbelievably irritating. I for one would happily take out
a contract on Daphne and CJ to negate their smugness,
possibly with the above mentioned wood chisel, whilst
Wendy would be more inclined have Chris removed
from the planet via a controlled explosion. Slightly
concerned that maybe we both need psychiatry for even
contemplating this misdemeanour, I have mentioned it
to a few others who completely agree with me.
Although the format of this program is quite ingenious
just about everybody I speak to is irritated by the team,
with Barry in his anorak and posh Judith also causing
fury to some. It appears that the only one of the team
any of us would actually have round for tea is Kevin but
I suspect even that may become boring after two
glasses of mineral water and a recital on the history of
Goa.

This time of year is ski season, although mine was
cut short yesterday after doing a rather impressive if not
acrobatic handstand on the slopes in the Pyrenean
mountains. I now have some strong strapping on my
right thumb as a result, which makes this keyboard a bit
of a challenge, let alone cooking and washing up.

It seems that despite spring attempting to show its
welcome face in the very near distance, winter is still
having one last kick at the ball here in mid March.
Today it is snowing, quite hard in fact. The shrubs that
had been misled into believing their dawn had arrived

and have started displaying shoots will be thoroughly disappointed this morning with the temperature at minus 4. I am guessing this may have a disastrous affect on the grape vines too, so perhaps you read it here first, '*French wine prices due to rocket in 2010*'. Nature can be so cruel sometimes, we may have to pay over £2 for a bottle next year! Maybe I should invest my home-made 5 gallons on the futures market? Anything would be better than drinking the foul stuff. So today is a time to sharpen up the chainsaw and stoke up the grate once more in a bid to keep warm. And to think I had shorts on most of last week. At least it gets me out of digging the veggie patch for a few more days, were it that I was capable of using a spade with one hand anyway.

Pipework and pooches

April 2010

I noticed last week that we have a slight issue with our downstairs bathroom. When we empty the bath the water goes down the plughole only to re-emerge in the middle of the room and I am not entirely convinced this is supposed to happen. So, after lifting the lino to see it rising from a crack in the floor, I make a feeble attempt to contain it with silicone. This inevitably failed miserably and it then turns into a geyser which rises a couple of feet in the air after the bath had been used and floods out into the sitting room. So I removed it. All of it. When is a bathroom not a bathroom? Well when it has no floor, walls, ceiling or plumbing I guess. And to make it worse, the original walls behind the walls are painted bright mauve. Whatever were those people on in the seventies? Who paints a bathroom mauve? So we are now up to our knees in concrete, pipework, plasterboard and tiles for the next few months until I have managed to re-install it all again. The bath itself meanwhile is sitting on the back lawn like something from Steptoe's yard, awaiting rain to fill it. The toilet and basin are alongside it too, so it looks like one of those pranks that students play on each other, the one where they remove the entire contents of a colleague's room and re-erect it on the bursar's lawn in a fit of drunken giggling. Although maybe they don't do that any more? Kids don't try this at home.

Talking of giggling, those of you who still read this column may remember that this time last year I mentioned our noisy frog population. Well, they are once again back in chorus, singing their happy songs in the rain. Except the rain is notably missing this year and we are unofficially in a drought. Perhaps by the time you read this it may have arrived in torrents but I swear we have had no more than a few droplets since New Year and the ground is as dry as a desert (or is that dessert? I get those two mixed up), with dust swirling in the breeze. The farmers already have their sprinkler systems working which I take as good indicator that no rain is imminent either, despite the forecast. Come to mention it, why is it that long range forecasts are so hopeless? We were threatened with wet weeks end-to-end a month or so ago, but every time I recheck it on the internet the storms have moved to next week in a sort of *jam tomorrow* fashion. I am sure my grandfather was 300 times more accurate in his weather forecasting using only a barometer and his intelligence as guide and without the aid of millions of pounds worth of satellite equipment or gormless weather girls with push button gadgets and too much makeup to relay it to us.

I am not sure of the exact meaning of the expression "hair of the dog", save to say it has something to do with alcohol indulgence, but I am sure someone in this publication can pinpoint its exact origins in the finest detail. However, in our house it's meaning is literal. We have two dogs, a scruffy collie-like thing which requires an annual haircut, one that will be postponed until later this spring after our escapade last year involving her needing a jacket. The other one, however, just sheds his hair all over the place, on the floor, the bed, the sofa, its everywhere. How can a medium sized gundog grow so much of the stuff, its amazing; we sweep up piles and piles of it. So much so that we are considering starting a cottage industry stuffing cushions with it and selling them at the *vide grenier*, France's equivalent of the car boot sale. Incidentally, the words *vide grenier* literally translate into 'empty attic' and that's what these things are, people emptying all their rubbish on to the gullible public, many of whom are Brits. There are enterprising old folks selling broken furniture and rusty nails and I am sure you could probably buy the cobwebs too if you bargained hard enough. But for some reason these weekly events are a magnet to some folks. We have friends who convene at a different one every Sunday breakfast time without fail, queuing up to hunt down the bargains. Some even so passionate that they take trailers so they can buy huge articles of junk to clutter their already over-cluttered houses with original French artefacts. OK I did buy a 1970's stereo amplifier at one last year, for a fiver, because I <u>needed</u> it after my last one suffered spontaneous combustion. Nevertheless that was *all* I purchased and I managed to resist buying anything rusty or smelling of mothballs at all.

Last weekend saw our annual trip to the dreaded "i" place, you know the one? Yep; IKEA. The sortee been discussed and planned for weeks beforehand and I had been living in dread, me not being the best at shopping at all, let alone in that god-awful place. I had dreamed up a million excuses why I couldn't make it, my poorly thumb, overwork, overslept, overpriced, I used them all but to no avail. So off we went at 7.30am on Saturday supposedly to beat the crowds. But no, it seems that everyone in the world goes early to beat the crowds, thus creating, well er, crowds. We did the usual shuffle around tramlined course buying loads of things that we didn't need and not finding the things we went for. We fathom out things with names like Humbidog, Halm, and Balm, in colours of light brown, mid brown and dark beige. Then we queue for 30 minutes while the student staff figure out how to work the cash-tills, probably because they are all in Swedish, it not being a common language in France. Eventually we *carry* all our unnecessary pile of booty to the van, which is parked 4 miles away, because the trolley wont fit through the narrow railings in case we steal it. But it isn't over then is it, because you get home and have to open all the packs there and then to immediately assemble all the damn stuff. I have never been good with instructions, usually reverting to the manly way of assembling things by intuition, preferably with a hammer in hand. How hard can it be? I know Sweden is a very organised and clean living country but one can't help wondering how many divorces there are in the world caused by assembling IKEA furniture? It seems I am the only one in our household who *prefers* the bookshelves upside down, I think they look great! If you ask me, the best thing in IKEA is the free pencils, I now have another 20 or more in my golf bag. That should last me another year until that traumatic pilgrimage comes around again. At least we have a shiny new toilet roll holder, but sadly have neither toilet nor wall to put in on. Back to work then.

Hang em high

May 2010

Another hectic month here at Chauffour has seen us under pressure to get things done and rooms finished before the arrival of quite a few guests for our annual party at the end of May. What started out a few years ago to be a small celebration of Wendy and I getting together seems now to have blown up into some sort of festival. There will definitely be tents, that's for sure.

Thankfully this extra busy schedule has helped us avoid getting bogged down with the recent UK elections campaign with its highly televised programmes depicting politicians touring the country kissing babies and smiling greasily for the camera. And how does it end? A stalemate, a hung parliament. Hang the lot of them I say?

Today is a national holiday, they seem to have a lot of these in France this time of year. This one celebrates VE day, I guess to remind France of the relief when the Germans gave them their country back after the last World War. Although this has now been a long time ago, traditions are deep in French culture and, unlike cosmopolitan UK, France is still by-and-large for the French, complete with its 2 hour lunch breaks and Monday closing. Things are changing however, with the infiltration of the Brits there is more demand for regularity. "We are all in Europe", we hear them cry, "so you must do as we do". Funny how the Brits can demand their constitutional rights overseas and yet have to kowtow to the requirements of immigrants in their own country? Anyway, the French commercial world must be listening because we now have a few supermarkets which stay open during lunchtime, so that if you haven't managed to organise your day to be at the shop before noon you can still get some bread. In fact our local shop and bakery have both recently changed hands and instead of "patron des miserables" with their minor opening hours consisting of a short stretch in the morning and quick *overt* in the afternoon, they now are staffed by youngsters and are open all day from 7 till 7. And guess what, they do a lot more business and possibly even make money as a result, so everyone wins. "Sacre bleu!" the older generation are grumbling into their claret, "they will be having drive-in Boulangeries next or heaven forbid, Sunday opening". The route into this century has finally arrived and is not just kicking and screaming, it's got steel toecaps and a megaphone.

I had a bath this morning, hurrah. You may recall that I had removed our bathroom in a fit of deranged panic last month and it has taken me until now to re-install it all. The last tile went on the wall yesterday to Wendy's quite vivid colour requirements. I don't do colour. OK, I can see primary colours but after that the variety of shades are just a blur to me and decisions on this matter are best left to others. For instance I was doing some work on a house recently and the owner required that we paint the shutters while we were on site. His wife wanted them a sort of *duck-egg* colour he told me on the phone, so could I go and buy some paint for him? When he came to view it he proposed that if a duck ever laid an egg that colour it must be extremely unwell! Fortunately his wife was also partial to turquoise so it all ended OK.

We now have a lodger. A friend and his wife had some matrimonial difficulties resulting in their parting of the ways. A 'friend in need' etc etc; we offered him a bed for a few weeks until he got himself sorted. After accepting our kind gesture he then proceeded to move a caravan into the garden, made himself at home and is currently enjoying the view so much he intends to stay until autumn. We shall have to see about that. Why is it that the Welsh are so thick skinned? I don't want to upset him though. I was reminded recently of another Welsh chap who, to settle a vendetta, sneaked round in the dead of night and put a thimble full of round-up in the guy's watering can. Those of you who know the mysterious powers of round-up will acknowledge that there may have been some despair a few weeks later when all his flowers faded to nothing. Now that *is* cruel. So *bienvenue*, mon ami, do enjoy your stay!

I mentioned last month that we have been in a drought for quite a while and predicted that things may change soon. Well they did, dramatically. The first few days in May were absolute scorchers, with temperatures up to nearly 30 before **wallop**, back down to earth we came with 6 degrees, miserable rain, more heating fuel and shivering dogs (yes, haircuts have been administered). Is this weather something to do with Iceland too? For a small country that place certainly seems to have a world impact. I had to put up with my son for 2 weeks because he couldn't fly back last month due to some cloud having the wrong sort of dust in it. They really shouldn't be so careless to let all this happen. I couldn't see Britain letting dangerous clouds out into the sky. They would have consultants in hard hats to advise them on that sort of thing. And it is doubtful the French would let it happen either, but if it did, well they would just take a few days holiday.

So this Iceland place has given us bankrupt councils, grounded airlines, erratic weather patterns and Magnus-bl**dy-Magnusson. Countries have been invaded and nuked for less!

Growing old?

June 2010

At what age does a man become interested in growing roses? For years I have noticed them but never really given them more than a passing glance. So why is it now, as I draw nearer to 50 years old that they suddenly fascinate me? Wendy recently bought me one called Cyrano de Bergerac, named after a local hero in these parts. It is now in full bloom with it's light yellow flowers so perfectly formed and, as we appear to be in monsoon season, it is growing so fast you can almost see it move as it smothers an outer wall on the terrace with colour. Now, as I wander through our garden I also see pink ones, apricot ones and startling red ones which are all part of the legacy of wilderness that we inherited with the house. It has taken nearly 3 years to get the place back to a reasonably groomed state and it must be that I have failed to notice these splendid blossoms in the past. That or they have only just decided to forgive me for the radical pruning that everything got 2 years ago.

It is now a couple of weeks since our annual party when 15 guests were somehow shoehorned into this house. Sadly the weather didn't offer any kindness this year apart from delivering a rather spectacular thunderstorm complete with dayglo flashing skies. Fortunately the leaking roof into one of the guest rooms was contained by means of a bucket which the particular guests were quite happy to empty on the hour. The feed trough was refilled 3 times per day mostly with the willing help of a volunteer or two and generally everyone mucked into make it a successful 6 days. On the night of the actual party a couple of guitar musicians turned up and tried to outdo each other with songs to suit all tastes. One even reverted to magic tricks to steal the show, providing a memorable display involving a cigarette and a lady's cashmere cardigan! He lived to tell the tale. But the best part is, for once, there was still some wine left in the cave when they all left. Bunch of lightweights eh…

We were given a gift of a set of boule, or petanque as it is known in there parts. Perhaps another sign that we must be aging or at least people think we are? Anyway, we looked up the rules and then gave it a go. For those of you uninitiated in this game, it involves throwing metal balls a few yards to try and settle them nearest to a smaller ball. Sort of like bowls only played on gravel with a very low skill level. The French play it for days on end but I have to say it is the most boring game since the 1973 finals of the *World Paint Drying* contest, unless of course you count watching England playing football last weekend…

They now have a shiny new air terminal at Bordeaux airport. Shiny, yes, new, yes. High tech, very much no. It has only recently opened and the day we flew there was a ceremony going on with suited dignitaries being shown around, polishing their egos and sipping free shampoo. What they failed to notice was the complete chaos that was happening. Four Easyjet female staff were ticking off hand written boarding cards on a list with a highlighter pen and then trying to balance the number of passengers on the paperwork, albeit unsuccessfully. It took over an hour. I did suggest that perhaps they should consider a computer for this purpose, as did most other airports, but it seems the airline has now gone all low tech, presumably to save money? I can only guess that some poor Mr Jones had been mistaken for Mr James and was unknowing en route to Glasgow instead of Luton, without his luggage. Meanwhile the rest of us were herded into a pen where we were forced to *stand* for further hour until the issue was resolved. So a new airline terminal without computers or seats? Or manners come to think of it. All hail the modern advances in airline travel, a new milestone has been reached.

Last weekend we were back in Rock for the first time in 6 months to coincide with some visiting relatives and a family gathering. While we were there I took the opportunity to show Wendy around Witley Court. It has been some years since I was last there and I have to admit it has changed a bit since the days when, as youngsters, we used to take a few bottles of cider and a radio to party on the front lawn until the early hours or wonder amongst the falling debris of the buildings. Now it is all spruced up and protected by cameras and we even had the aid of a audio player to tell us it's intimate history. Needless to say we now had to pay £6 to enter but I have to admit that the fountain display was spectacular as were the newly revamped gardens and it was a nice afternoon out. I was reminded by my father that as a young chap his father drove him and his sisters to Great Witley to watch the place burning down in 1937. The things they did for entertainment before the invention of TV eh? He also regaled a tale of grandfather visiting Witley court for dinner at the invitation of the owner, one Herbert (piggy) Smith, some years earlier to discuss settlement of some outstanding accounts that the man owed him. It seems that they sat either end of a massive table each being served by separate butlers. The table that was set for 2 was so large that conversation was impossible without the aid of a megaphone and grandfather left afterwards still without managing to collect his money!

On Sunday morning we were heading to the airport when we reached a traffic jam of metropolitan proportion, causing us to take 45 minutes to cover a 2 mile stretch towards Ombersley and thus nearly missing our flight. When we eventually reached the problem obstacle, it was just a couple of traffic cones cordoning off part of the island around a manhole but it was controlled by a 4 way set of traffic lights causing absolute mayhem. Why is it that Sunday drivers, in their moronic mundane states, just accept this as normal, quite happy to while away the hours in their cars? In France, one of the drivers would have jumped out, removed the offending cones, unplugged the lights and let the traffic flow. Except that in France they wouldn't need to, as when there was nobody working on the site (eg night time or weekends) the contractors would pull the barriers to one side to allow cars to pass each other slowly and with a little intelligence. Hmm, does the word intelligence apply to British Sunday drivers, je ne pense pas? And possibly not to government contractors either. Je despair!

Parisian and London Riviera
July 2010

Earlier in the month we took a few days at the sea, on the beautiful small island of Ile de Re, just off the Atlantic coast near La Rochelle. The small harbour town of St Martin was magnificent, with its rows of chic little restaurants all serving fresh seafood and interspersed with trendy boutiques selling designer clothes at extortionate prices. The harbour was full of yachts as there was a regatta on that weekend, but not the vulgar billionaire ones that one sees on the Mediterranean, more those of the understatedly wealthy. The sort of wealth that said, "Yes, I do have a Ferrari, but I keep mine out of sight round the back". The general tourists travelled around on bikes, despite the 30+ degree heat and cobbled streets but we declined that adventure, deciding on the cooler air conditioned car option to take in the other villages on the island. We came across some very shaggy coated donkeys unlike any I have seen before, which apparently are native to the island. Not only do they have shaggy coats but when they are working in the salt flats they are also fitted with pyjamas! I kid you not, pink and blue check no less, something to do with keeping the salt off their skin. Now, of course, the animals are no longer used for work in this way but just flaunt their night attire to the hoards of wealthy Parisians who have recently adopted this island as their playground. It seems the whole of Paris descends on the island each weekend and their clamouring to purchase property has driven prices to monumental heights. A 25 sq m apartment in St Martin will set you back over quarter of a million euros, that's nearly 10,000 per square metre, Paris or London prices. Come to think of it, the price of a nice meal would nearly buy you a property where we live.

While we were there we watched the England football team inevitably crash out to the Germans in a bar with only one other person in it, who happened to be a German. I have to say it was a relief when we lost, in the same way that a myxi rabbit would be relieved to be put out of its misery or a dying fly be squashed under a leather sole. Then two days later, after all the St Georges car flags had been replaced with Union Jacks (Murray being a Scot), our tennis hero was once again defeated in his sport. At least he played well and went out to the world number one though. I am relieved to say that in France we have never seen one flag flying in aid of sport, despite the French being fairly good at quite a few of them. Why do the Brits (aided by the press) manage to whip themselves up into such a frenzy, only to come crashing back down again, whilst other nations just enjoy sport for what it is? It beats me. I am a great advocate of the power of belief but have always thought it a lot easier when coupled with a little intelligence.

We found ourselves back in UK again later this month, this time in aid of charity. A friend of ours is an ex-international rowing coxswain and he had been asked to cox a team of rowers in an event to raise money for Alzheimer's disease. One of his compatriots had been diagnosed with the disease in 2007 and who is now nearing an advanced stage, had organised an eight man crew to row 20 miles, upstream through 7 locks, from Eton to Henley to coincide with the Henley Royal Regatta. I had been asked to take official photographs of the event. We turned up at Boulter's Lock in Maidenhead for breakfast to witness them coming through the lock, in itself no mean feat in a 20 metre shell with oars that only just fit within the walls. It was here that I met Jamie Graham whose family had organised the event and who was intending to row the whole way despite his condition. When you meet someone like this you witness the tragedy that this disease can inflict, himself such a great rower and athlete; it was heart breaking. My cousin was at school with him and had asked me to send on his regards. I squirmed as Jamie tried his hardest to recall him but it was obvious that not only had this memory faded but pretty much all other memories had as well. I could have cried for this man.

Anyway, we progressed on to Henley regatta in our best bib and tucker where I realised that my plain blue blazer was menially ordinary amongst the bright coloured stripes of those from the rowing fraternity. We did our best to blend in by using the word "spiffing" quite a lot and introducing ourselves as Lord & Lady Chauffour (it's in France don't you know, *snort*!) to anyone who portrayed a condescending manor. One ruddy faced old buffer in a ridiculous pink and green hat even said he had heard of it! The very tired VIII man crew, with an even more tired coxswain, eventually arrived down the Henley straight accompanied by a launch on which stood a lone piper, piping. As it passed the grandstand we cheered from the bank like a homecoming parade as though our own world cup winning team had returned victorious. We were (and always will be) proud to play a minor part in this monumental achievement. Through their website www.forgetmenotrow.com their efforts have thus far raised over £65,000 for Alzheimer's research. I am not one to push charities on anyone but please pay it a visit if you get chance.

Now back in France we are experiencing the long awaited summer that has been lacking over the past few months. The combines have been gobbling up the wheat crops in what is predicted to be a record harvest and the trees are once again laden with fruit. I have already made the first chutney of the year, a cheeky little number made from excess courgettes and windfall apricots. My attention has turned to the rebuilding of the barn wall that collapsed in January after that extraordinary frost, as the insurance have finally settled (only 50%) after a 6 month wrangle to do with our not fulfilling our responsibility to turn off the water supply.

So now, far removed from the splendours of upper class culture, I am back to wielding a shovel in the 30 degree heat and mixing concrete and pickles. Please spare me no sympathy.

Mr and Mrs Tomato

August 2010

Mid summer in rural France is a time for the country fete and boy do they know how to do these. Every small community has its own, some more than one per year. Our community has only 500 residents yet it's 'Fete et Foulees Gauloise' held last weekend was a classic example of how the rural community is so bound together. The 20 page free colour booklet gives details of all the activities on offer including a 12km walk of which 60-70 folks trooped past our door at 9am on Saturday morning. Their were also bike rides, quad bike trails, fishing competitions, a marathon run, art and sculpures. The whole thing culminated in a huge *repas*, a meal for upwards of 1000 people, all seated and fed with 4 courses including a whole steer which was spit roasted in the middle of the square. A disco and music festival followed with 2-3000 people present of all ages which went on till daybreak. Quite unbelievable for a village half the size of Rock, and to think that the next village only a few miles away would hold a similar event on a different weekend.

The festival that was held the previous weekend in our nearest town of Marmande was altogether more sinister though, none other than the renowned TOMATO festival. I had read that on the Friday there was an annual wedding, that of Mr and Mrs Tomato themselves, but sadly we were unable to attend. Shame, because Wendy was looking forward to getting some ideas for an outfit when her turn comes! We did however make our usual trip to the Saturday morning market, which had been doubled in size to include traders offering multiple varieties of tomatoes and a free tasting. I should point out that the Marmande variety of tomato is rather famous and possible the most tasty in the world. What we were unprepared for was the initiation ceremony that we also witnessed, welcoming some new members to the worshipful masterful fraternity of the tomato. It went as follows:

1. A crowd of elder statesmen of the 'order of the tomato' assembled on a stage with their long gowns emblazoned with red and green wearing hats resembling lampshades.

2. They were then joined by some younger (and more active) members of the Order, complete with their large round tomato hats.

3. There were a few tomato verses read out before two rather nervous looking men were ushered to the front of the stage in their civilian clothes. First they were made to drink some potion which one would suspect was in fact tomato juice although some of the elders may just have earned the right to 'bloody Mary' theirs up a bit.

4. The new comers were then presented with their tomato robes and had to read and then sign an ancient parchment scroll. Sadly I was unable to translate their

French fast enough to know exactly what their commitment entailed, so I have to improvise here, but I am guessing it went along the lines of *"I herby declare my allegiance and commitment to maintain the welfare of the hallowed tomato and swear my allegiance to all tomatokind...etc etc"*.

5. Once this was complete there was a quick munching of few tomatoes slices and then off to the pub. It was all deadly serious and most bizarre.

I was a little concerned that the chairman of the tomato council (for I am again guessing that was his title) wore mirrored sunglasses and looked extremely shady. I couldn't help wondering that after being a good guy by day he spent his evenings sacrificing virgins in an underground candlelit greenhouse somewhere, chanting evil verses and wearing the head of a tomato with tiny horns on it a la Christopher Lee in Hitchcock's film 'To the devil a daughter'!

France has once again reinforced it's stance on patriotism to the world by voting overwhelmingly to ban the wearing of the Islamist burka in public. The huge majority in the house of parliament of 335 <u>for</u> the bill and only one <u>against</u> (possibly a Muslim) not only highlights the sense of democracy that the French government is trying to re-establish but also the state of the government assembly itself. For example, as the house has 557 seats, one assumes the remaining 221 members were either on holiday the day the bill was voted in, which is quite possible, or more likely they held a difference of opinion but were frightened to put their vote forward for fear of being outcast? Democracy at its finest, you must agree? Although I hold no personal opinion on the subject I do admit that they should maybe ban the wearing of this garment whilst driving a car, the French are bad enough at that without needing blinkers.

We now at last have some more sheep, 4 that we bought from a friend. Unfortunately she had already named them. *Ma* has curly horns and is of indefinable origins, *Pa* is some sort of Charollais breed with a long tail and exceptionally large testicles and the other two ewes are just known as White and Blue respectively. Ma likes stale bread so we're told. We were unwilling to also purchase their offspring, called **Lamb**rusco, **Lamb**retta, **Lamb**orghini and **Lamb**ada, partly because I would feel rather foolish calling them by name and partly because they are fat enough now for the freezer and we don't have enough space this year. I am always wary of applying names to animals that are destined for the table, it is guaranteed to end in tears when the time comes. I can still recall the sad day as a 9 year old when my pet lamb, Flopsy, went off to that big white fridge in the sky as did Oinky-grub and Apple Sauce, my favourite free range pigs a year later. It was at least a week before I ate pork again after that one.

I had another birthday again recently. I don't particularly like birthdays, I find them laborious and unnecessary to anyone over the age of 10. However, I did this year enjoy a present of an electric gadget for zapping mosquitoes. Although I am not in favour of naming farm animals I felt this appliance did require a name. So Frank Zappa now lives on our terrace, doing his job with satisfying regularity. If this name sounds mysterious to you, then ask somebody male, in their early fifties, with a chequered past, possibly sporting a pony tail and an earring.

Football and the Black sea

September 2010

The summer is closing on us now although our grass is still awaiting rain to give it its proper colour back. We try to sneak an annual holiday in this time of year, choosing to go when the majority of tourists have given up and gone home. As I get older I find less attraction in holidaying with tourists I neither know or like, and prefer it when the weather has cooled a bit and the autumn colours are starting to show.

So to start with we spent a few days in Rock, taking in the annual Rock show while we were there, always an annual international attraction. We witnessed the ongoing vegetable contest, where prizes for exceptional produce were divided up between Tom Bore and Austin Fletcher in almost equal proportions. I was roped into play for the local Old Rockers against some very nimble young opposition in a game of football. I will admit that football is not my game and this became very evident as I did my best to keep goal, a position that simultaneously allowed me to finish my pint of Guinness. I would like to thank the rest of the old rockers for keeping the ball away from our goal mouth for most of the game, despite their failing health and fitness; that did help restrict us to a commendable 3-1 loss. I am also rather glad we avoided the need to use the air ambulance, particularly as the good people of Rock had raised a fine sum for their charity only the week before. I hope Jess and the two Daves in particular are managing to walk on two legs again by the time this goes to print. My mother pointed out that I was not the first Frazier to play in the local Rock team, herself turning out for the "married" against "single" ladies in 1983, again playing in goal, in a mini skirt. She didn't remember the score, just the skirt.

The farm was in full action, harvest gathered but not yet sold, next years crop's going underground as the cycle repeats itself once more. I did my bit for the cause, thirty minutes on the tractor pulling a roller to help out. It made me smile. Many a girlfriend has sat on my tractor mudguard over the years as Wendy did this time, intrigued with the workings of a local farm and it's machinery. But I will admit, never before have I driven a tractor fitted with a reclining driver and passenger seats complete with seatbelts. What purpose these will serve baffles me, were they really necessary for my well being? Would they protect me from a shunt at 6 miles per hour in a 4 ton machine? Or is this one more example of bureaucracy once again going a step too far? I have not yet established whether this sublime ruling is in force in France but I may possibly return home to receive a summons to fit seatbelts to my 1971 Ford 3000 tractor, or my garden mower even. I somehow doubt it.

While we were at Coningswick my father recalled a tale of a military plane crashing nearby during the early years of the war. He vividly remembers an Ambro Hanson catching the electric wires and coming down near the brickyard corner at Abberley. He raced to see the wreckage which had swiftly been cordoned off in military fashion. As far as he is aware, the whole thing was hushed up and no record of it ever kept or published. He did claim a souvenir though, as would most boys in that situation, one of its dials. Unfortunately this has been lost, but we all would be interested to know if anyone else recalls this incident? Perhaps the editor would be pleased to hear from you, unless of course this information is still withheld under the official secrets act (Rock edition).

From Rock we headed to Bulgaria, from where I write, watching the waves from my small apartment in a quiet holiday complex by the Black Sea. I am wondering at the state of this economy, with its dirty money, grubby tourists, sordid nightclubs and potholed roads. As with the rest of the world, the recession has hit here, with rows of unfinished concrete sprawling holiday complexes scarring the once bleak shores, many with no hope of ever being completed. When I first purchased this place 7 years ago it was a land of Dreams, sadly now, those dreams have been broken for so many, the majority of developers throwing in the towel and walking away from their responsibilities to fulfil the supply of those dream homes. The locals are now clinging to the hope that the Russians are coming with new money, coming to snap up the apartments and bring long awaited finances and a quick turn around in fortunes. Personally I cannot see it reviving the property market and I think it will be a few years yet before Bulgaria cleans up its act and revives it economy.

Still, can't complain, this property is away from the tourist track, the sun is high and living is cheap, lager less than a £1 per pint. Cheers.

We head from here to Scotland next week, up in the West Highlands, again by the shore, only with bigger waves and midges. We both love Scotland, its tranquillity a great tonic, even for us who live in a very rural area. The west coast has always been a draw for me, since those long gone days when I used to attend the highland cattle sales at Oban. In my younger days I was a cattle hairdresser. Yes I know that is hard to believe, especially as my own mop now resembles that of a highland cow itself. But in those days I was ahead of the game and took many commissions to clip cows near and afar, including Australia, Canada and America. One of my more famous works, (famous to those in the cow clipping fraternity that is) was to give a demonstration of clipping a highland cow at the opening of the new Oban cattle market in 1992. The market was opened by none other that HRH the Princess Royal who came along to witness this expert coiffure in action. It would appear that neither she nor the animal in question were very impressed with my efforts, HRH chastising me for taking away the animals traditional character and the latter reiterating her views by showing its traditional character and kicking hell out of me. My knighthood never arrived in the post, I suspected it wouldn't.

Meanwhile back at home we have news on the pet front. Followers of this column may recall that over a year ago our resident cat decided to leave home, to where and for reasons unknown. Well, we were coming home from the bar one night last week when Wendy demanded that I stopped the car from which she leapt and delved into the undergrowth of a sunflower field. Fearing she was the worse for drink, I patiently waited for her return in silence. A few minutes later she was back in her seat and we continued our journey home, her mumbling something about a cat. You can imagine my surprise when said cat joined in our conversation from the back seat. So now we are all reunited, it purring in our living room once more and stealing food from the kitchen. It would appear that its two daughters, which we still have in residence, refuse to welcome it home and there have been moments of fur flying, but Wendy seems overjoyed that our Madge has returned. Only time will tell if she chooses to stay, especially as we are away for a couple of weeks now. My guess is that she may head off to be reunited with whoever was feeding her a better class of kittycat than we do, once she has eaten the mound of tinned food we have left her with in our absence. At least we are comforted that she is alive and well.

Grand chutney

October 2010

Peace at last. No, not from any wars, no treaty, just an empty house. I enjoy having a houseful of people and maybe we do entertain a bit too well and make everyone too welcome, but in the end even I can run out of steam. So, as possibly our last visitor this summer left last weekend, I finally get chance to sit down and catch up, indoors obviously, I missed the sunshine while I was doing the washing up! The list of jobs that has mounted up is endless: fix the heating, chop logs, replace broken roof tile and general rugging up for another winter; they all lie in wait, but wait they can, for a few more days anyway. The rain has finally arrived at Chauffour with vengeance and, judging by our pond being over 3 metres lower than it should be, there will inevitably be a long period of top up. Rural France doesn't really do winter, in the way that Greenland doesn't do swimming pools or Iraq has no snow cannons. Everything just goes dead. Bars and restaurants adopt their random winter opening hours, each without reason or warning, although I am sure they just close when they see me coming round the corner. Many expats head South to Spain or home to UK, to escape the cold winters we endure here in the absence of the help of the warming gulf stream. When in north Scotland earlier in the month, nobody believed me that they get warmer winters up there than we do.

Talking of golf, that's another thing I don't get enough time for any more. I did take time to watch the first day of the Ryder Cup live from Cardiff though, in fact friends of mine from here even went to it that day, all the way from France. Yes, the very day it rained 6 inches of water onto the fairways. The day was cancelled and instead I believe they played a water polo match on the 16th green! It all worked out in the end though, a great result for team Europe.

Last year we organised a new annual event, that of the Aquitaine Chutney Festival. Sadly last years' was cancelled due to family illness, but this year, the second (technically the first) event did take place and I am happy to report it was a rip roaring success. Well unfortunately not a success for my jars of preserves as I only managed a couple of second prizes, one with my apricot and courgette sweet pickle and one with a jam. I did win the prize for 'product with the best name' though, my 2009 white wine entitled 'SCREAM!' won that. I have to admit, it is screamingly horrible and the judge agreed. The overall champion, from 35 entries, was sweet thai sauce from Vanessa, a professional chutney-maker from miles away, and runner up was my neighbours sweet sherry. Both were quite nice. If you like that sort of thing!

France has now invented a new sport called "Spot-the-Romanian", a game for all the family. You can have hours of fun sneaking around the vineyards or back streets of rural areas and if you see what you think may be a Eastern European gypsy, basically anyone with gold earrings larger that 3cms in diameter, you take a discrete photo with your mobile phone and text it to the immigration police. You then wait for the cavalry to arrive, complete with tear gas and taser guns, who beat the suspect to a pulp before they package them up and ship them back to Romania from the nearest post office. Well it's not exactly like that, but our President has definitely started a witch hunt on immigrants in France. Maybe he will be sending the Brits home next. Good idea, lets arrest anyone wearing sandals and socks. Je suis Monsieur Francais!

Yet more news on the cat front at our place, the old cat has left, been found, left again and since returned. As the winter arrives, so do the mice, so the cat leaves to get Whiskers somewhere else. Maybe she is just scared of mice? Je despair. Time to load up the traps once more.

Many of you, young and old, will know of the whirlwind phenomenon that is Facebook.com. For the uninitiated, it is an internet website where people can interact with their friends online. It is in fact an extremely addictive internet website where you pretend to be friends with loads of people, including that bloke you once met in a pub and exchanged emails with but cannot remember what he looked like. Then you have competitions with your mates to see who has the most Facebook friends, when you only really have one, your own brother. You post up daily snippets of what you are doing or where you have been, regardless of whether they may be interesting or not. So why is it so engaging? Do I really care that a past friend of mine called Sally is off to feed her cows, or that some bloke called Ollie had a great night out in Leeds, complete with pictures of him and some drunken girls taken on his phone at 3am? And what is worse are all those unfunny comments underneath, followed by the word 'LOL'. Laugh out loud? Cringe-out-loud more like! And then there are all those stupid games on there too, where people keep sending me gifts. I received a piglet the other day, for my pretend farm, which I don't want but can't get rid of! But then some days, driven by who-knows-what, I suddenly feel compelled to announce to the world that I have just planted my seed potatoes or made a rather nice pot of jam. Then I post photos on facebook of my holidays, in hopes that someone will add a comment on how nice it all looks or how sweet our animals are. Have we all gone mad? Does anyone care about that stuff? Simple answer. No they don't. They are just bored. Whatever next, people will be writing articles in local parish magazines about their mundane daily existence. COL!

The Pointless pointer

November 2010

Is it me, or does time just go by in a whir these days? No sooner its Monday then the weekend looms. No sooner I get up than its time to think about bed. No sooner I write this monthly article than a copy of Rock News drops onto my doormat, signalling the end of yet another month, dammit. No sooner its January then old Scrooge here thinks of ways he can avoid Christmas this year. What to do this time? I have tried hiding, staying in bed, even being blind drunk, but none of these afford me the luxury of escaping those goddam annoying jingles that signify the arrival of the bearded bloke in the bright suit. No not Noel Edmonds, the other one.

Last year I gave a mention to some mysterious looking facial hair cropping up on the top lips of some celebrities and sportsmen around this time of year. This month I have gone one further and joined the **Movember** ranks myself and grown a 'mo' for the charity that raises awareness of men's health issues. So if you see me around, or anyone else sporting an out-of-character moustache give them a few quid for their efforts. Thanks.

The late autumn at Chauffour brings us ripening apples. Louis, our (pointless) pointer, likes apples. In fact he likes them so much that he lies by the door and whines all day, a whine like a whistling kettle that goes right through you, until he is let out to go and eat as many as he can before we can stop him. An apple-a-day may keep the doctor away, but a crate-a-day can only involve some hefty vet's bills. It did this time last year. He doesn't just eat them either; he engages some sort of bizarre antic which involves him throwing them in the air and jumping about like a lunatic beforehand. I never have considered that he is quite the full-shilling, but it seems he has at last lost the plot altogether. A mad March hare is a sight to behold, but nothing compared to a crazy autumn sub-normal canine with a single figure IQ, doing an apple-dance. Maybe we should send a video in to 'Animals-do-stupid-stuff' or whatever that programme is called. Or possibly the X-Factor! Come to think of it, Simon Cowell would probably give him a record deal.

The time has come round again to give worming tablets to the animals. In the olden days this was always a tricky job as even the dimmest of animals wouldn't eat a nasty tasting small pill. But nowadays it's all changed as some bright scientist has realised that if you make the tablet taste nice, any animal will eat it. Except ours! Louis the pointless pointer, no problem, he will eat anything; but the scruffy one with the brains, no chance. She was suspicious from the off, noticing a packet being opened while we pretended not to look at her. First tablet she took outside and buried it in the garden. Next one, sprinkled in her dinner, persuaded her that she wasn't hungry that day. Hold her down, shove it in, out it comes. Wrap it up in some tasty cooked meat, out it comes. A nightmare? Well, to anyone who has this problem, I can now reveal the solution. *Simply give it to the cat.* How dare the cat have something she hasn't got? Dog stole it and wolfed it down in an instant. Job done. I really should charge for this ingenious information.

I note last week the announcement of the Lonely Planet awards, in which the Shetland Islands were the winners. Now there's a surprise? You really couldn't get anywhere much lonelier that there surely, with possible exception of Greenland or a summer day in the House of Commons. So what are these awards about? When reading in more detail, it actually says that this is one of the **top regions in the world to visit next year**, according to their new guidebook. Have these people ever been there? Underneath this statement is a description of the place which says, and I quote: *"...a collection of mighty, wind-ravaged clumps of brown and green earth rising from the frigid waters of the North Sea..."* Well, I'll just go and pack then shall I? Should I take an overcoat do you think? My experience of Shetland is a complete absence of trees and vegetation, women with long grey hair, spinning wheels and goats. All from Yorkshire or Norfolk; except possibly the goats.

Does anyone get chance to watch Jamie Oliver's 30 minute meals on early evening TV? We do most evenings. 30 minutes they may well be, if you happen to have all that stuff in your fridge and at least a dozen pots of herbs growing on your windowsill. 30 minutes cooking, but how long shopping first? And what about the cost? "*Lets take some caviar, a whole lump of fresh parmesan cheese, some prime fillet steak and fresh guava fruit...and stir it up with this lovely spoon...*". 30 minute meals? 30 quid meals more like! And while we are at it, let's use every pan in the kitchen, along with a few gadgets. What I want to know is who does the washing up? And how long does it take? A damn sight longer than 30 minutes I bet!

The time has also come round for the opticians. Our old French farmhouse is designed to be cool in the summer, by having thick walls and very few windows. This time of year it is not only cold but, in a word, dark. Reading by firelight may sound romantic to some, but as age creeps up on me, I find **halogen** is the only way to go. As I type, I have a set of spotlights arranged around my keyboard like some sort of studio film set. But sadly the eyes are still straining. So a trip to the friendly optician in the local French town was required. Friendly, well she was certainly smiling as she relieved me of 150 euros for a pair of reading glasses. She will probably send me a Christmas card now; I'll pretend I cant read it!

For the last few months in this column I have banged on about the weather in this part of the world. More specifically, that we were expecting rain any day, and last month I gaily announced that it had arrived. Not so. We had one days drizzle and then back to the lovely dry days once more. If we were in UK I am sure this would by now have sparked a panic hosepipe ban, but here nobody seems too bothered, except our fish.

With only half a metre of water left in a 4 metre deep pond, the thousand strong shoal are having a bit of a housing issue. Apparently, during such crowded times, they eat each other! There you go, Grant Shapps, your UK housing problems solved in an instant. I really should be in politics!

Auction marts and blondes with attitude

November 2010

A long while ago I remember having a conversation with John Thorley, secretary of the National Sheep Association about more and more animals being sold on the dead weight. At the time, an advocate direct sales, I defended the birth of the new on-farm stock selection system and 'buying groups' trading direct with slaughterhouses. John's argument was that we should always maintain the use of the livestock auction system and that auction was the only true way of setting a market price. He also went on to wax on about how great the auction mart system was in UK and that we were the only country in Europe to have this benefit. At the time I argued that the auction system was outdated, with too many middlemen taking a financial cut out of the end product.

Some 20 years later I find myself living on a smallholding in rural France where they do not have the luxury of a local mart and I have to say that it one of the few things I miss about the UK. At the very least, it is a social gathering of like minded souls. Having been a pedigree sheep breeder all my life, I spent over year looking for our first sheep purchases. Eventually, through contact from friend of a friend we visited an old boy who had been breeding Charmoise sheep, some 50 kms away. He had little understanding of English and my schoolboy French, although improving year on year, was not up to translating the intimate details of gigot, muscle depth and bone ratios. We did a deal, me doing my best to keep the price down, but I have to say I had absolutely no idea what these animals were worth and am sure I paid over the odds.

Sadly, the sheep were killed a year later by stray dogs, a day we would rather forget. After a while, I was on the lookout again for more stock, but how? If I was back in UK, I would pop down to the mart once a week for a few weeks, to get an idea of prices, make some contacts and possibly pick up what I required. I cannot do that here and have ended up buying a mishmash of 3 ewes and a charollais ram from a friend who was struggling to look after them.

I am also on the lookout for a heifer, just something plainly bred but with a bit of shape. The farms around here are all stocked with Blonde d'Aquitaine and, at the risk of upsetting a few people, I don't like them, with their *long legs and bad attitude*. I would prefer to pick up a Limousin from the region 3 hours up the road, which I intend to cross with imported angus semen to breed an annual cross calf for the freezer. I am finding this task virtually impossible. Yes I could go to their annual pedigree sale and buy one for a few thousand but that is not within my budget. My only chance is to go knocking on doors to see if they have stock for sale. As you can well imagine, and Englishman doing this on a French farm is not the more cost effective way of trading.

So, in reflection, John Thorley, you absolutely are correct when you say that the auction mart is the backbone of the UK livestock industry. From time to time, farmers in UK may need to be reminded of this.

Heading North for winter

December 2010

As winter sets in firmly in our district in France, this year Wendy and I have decided to spend some of it in Scotland. My reasoning is, if we are going to have some winter, let's have some real winter. Logical? Well possibly not. After a very long drive we are now ensconced in a small cottage by the sea near Edinburgh, one that is well insulated with instant heating. For once a house that is toasty warm. Outside there is currently a foot of snow and I am maybe considering this decision to be a wee bit rash. But then taking the dogs for a run on the beach, stopping for a pint of real ale in a cosy pub with an open fire on the way back, having a chat to a neighbour; these are a few things that have been denied to us of late so it all makes a refreshing change. I am also using the time to write another novel.

A long drive through France will inevitably find you taking a quick stop at one of its motorway service stations. A service station that does what it is designed to do. A pleasantly attractive cashier, well dressed, with bright eyes and a gleaming smile welcomes you in. Inside you can sort through an array of snacks at reasonable prices, get a hot beverage and use the toilet facilities. You can sift through a small selection of magazines about general subjects such as motoring, gardening and fishing. One magazine entitled

"Tampons, made easy" did make me raise an eyebrow, but seemingly it was just something to do with painting. I will admit, that while drinking our coffee I noticed that the lady next to me sported a nice Louis Vuiton bag out of which was poking the head of a small bug eyed dog. But the French can surely be excused that little vice, the one that allows them to wear pets as a fashion accessory? All in all, I have to say that a motorway service station in France is a reasonably pleasant and quite painless experience.

However….having made it on to UK soil, the time came once more to stop into a service station, to let out our dogs to stretch their legs etc. So I thought I would make a few observations for a comparison.

The first thing you notice is the lack of pleasant staff, it appears that these places only offer employment to the under-educated rotund creatures who would be a shoe-in for a part in Stephen Spielberg's next horror movie. The ill-fitting cheap uniforms and baseball caps add a certain status to these people, relieving them of any sense of dignity they may once have had, along with any sense of humour and manners. I am drawn into the grossly over priced WH Smith store where I am confronted with huge racks full of so many magazines it would take me a week just to read all the titles. Someone should publish a magazine for magazine buyers, one that might guide me towards a suitable selection from the thousands on offer. I am baffled as to who buys all this stuff, glossy publications with titles such as 'Airfix for amateurs' and "Britain's next tin-opener". To pass the time, I consider what may interest me and decide perhaps something about tractors might suffice, me being the owner of a vintage model Ford. After some desperate searching I glance up to that forbidden top shelf, you know the one where all the illicit ladies dare to bare flesh on the front cover? Low and behold, I see it, 'Classic Tractor' nestled between 'Big Boobs' and 'Tickle fetish'. Since when has a tractor magazine contained adult content? Why oh why did they have to place it up there? I dare not reach up for it in case of being spotted. I am so shocked, my embarrassment colours my face red as I sidle away empty handed avoiding glares from old ladies branding me as a pervert.

I am amazed at the size of the huge shopping mall and attempt to head in the direction of something to eat. I negotiate my way through women leaping out at me proffering leaflets on subjects such as 'socialising with god' or 'saving a small Ugandan child from starvation'. I reply in French and they let me pass. I reach the drinks outlet aptly named Costa. Costa-packet by the looks of it. I am completely baffled by the endless list of variations on a simple cup of coffee. Latte and Cappuccino with added spices such as vanilla, basil and chilli. They come in different sizes, small, medium or 3 gallon bucket size that would keep me awake for about 4 years. In France, *un café* is a sufficient order, here the choice is so vast that I consider heading back to the magazine racks to buy a copy of 'Ordering coffee for beginners' to help me with my choice.

"YES?" barks the immigrant waitress, "Umm, I am still making up my mind" I mumble, embarrassed once again. She ignores me and moves on to the more savvy customer behind me who smugly orders a cocktail of various coffee beans and sophisticated additives. Totally confused, my appetite for coffee disappears and I move on in search of food.

A neon sign for Burgerland draws me into a booth where once again I am faced with a choice of a million variations on a standard beef-burger. I choose an Angus burger which arrives instantly. It is the size of a small family car. Once more a barrage of questions which defy logic come hurtling in my direction. '*Would I like a meal?*' I am asked. 'Uhh, OK' I reply, wondering what the other options might be. '*Would I like to GO LARGE?*' What? What could be larger than this? Cathedral size perhaps? With extra lard and a 4 acre field of potato chips? I decline and my server looks quite disappointed. Judging by his physique he has 'gone large' a few too many times himself as his sausage-like fingers count out my miniscule change.

I sit on the spindly chair trying to negotiate my feast, spurts of purple sauce flying out in all directions as I attempt to bite into it, grease dripping down my shirt. The bread has a similar consistency to the box it comes in. One bite is enough for me. If it was Angus, then I suspect it was from an Angus cow that had probably died of old age or possibly anorexia. I eat the chips and head back for the car. As I pass the nice Ugandan lady I offer the remnants of my burger for her to give to this poor starving child she is campaigning about. In fact I go one step further and suggest to her that if she gathers up all the left over angus-burgers from the nearby stall, in no time at all her poor starving child would soon be as fat as Idi Amin or whichever terrorist is running that country these days.

After a 17 hour journey, we arrived in Rock to stay for a few days. Any of you who frequent the Rock Cross Inn will have noted it now has new proprietors who have settled in quickly and are doing a roaring meal trade. I wish them all the very best. You may also have noticed that the pub has lost one of its loyal customers too, that of a canine variety. Sadly Honey, Val Frazier's friendly dachshund passed away earlier this month aged 13.

Before heading to Scotland, we visited the Royal Welsh winter fair in Builth Wells. It had been 10 years since I was last there and my mission was to do a bit of promotion for my new book amongst a few of my old cattle showing mates. We certainly picked an interesting day to go, our picturesque drive through the snowy Welsh mountains was stunning. However, I considered the car's thermometer to be malfunctioning when it decreased down to eleven degrees below freezing. Until we stepped outside that is. Apparently earlier that morning it had been minus 17! The rows of cattle and sheep were quite well prepared for this weather in their winter jackets. Two underdressed people just arriving from South France were definitely not. Fortunately there was an enterprising stall selling thermal socks and hats to help us through and we had a nice day. What I did find different after a ten year absence is the amount of people who now speak Welsh. It seems that it has been a compulsory subject in schools for a while which in its self is possibly a good thing, upholding tradition and all that. But why speak it constantly in public, is this strictly necessary? Come to think of it, what use is speaking Welsh anyway? Would it not be more productive for a small country, one that has little to offer other than sheep, to speak a more universally accepted language if it is to succeed in the modern world? Am I the only one who believes that this blinkered approach is very much a retrograde step for a country campaigning for its independence? The European banks are already bailing out Ireland, will it be Wales next?

Whilst there I picked up on an article relaying a speech from Wales's newly appointed Rural Affairs Minister, Elin Jones, which I read in disbelief. I will quote it directly.

"I want Welsh agriculture to be a modern industry. I want Welsh farmers on their tractors listening to Lady GaGa on their ipods and comparing beef cost-to-price ratios on their ipads in the local mart," she told NFU Cymru's annual conference.

Excuse me? Has she ever met a Welsh farmer? All the ones I know wouldn't know an i-pod from a pea pod! And the only GaGa Lady they will ever listen to is you madam. And not for very long either!

Ou est le Pain

December 2010

Living in France for 5 years now, bread is one thing that is taken for granted. We pop to the Boulanger every morning and pick up a crusty French loaf that has been baked on the premises that day and still warm. We generally don't eat the whole loaf fresh and the remainder of it is either blended up for breadcrumbs or fed to the animals. We have a couple of bird tables and 3 sheep and a pond full of hungry fish so it always gets used. Everybody in France does the same.

In contrast, the UK has one of the lowest bread consumptions in Europe. By comparison the bread here is awful at the very best of times, all pre-packed, already a few days old and tasteless. It goes stale after about 10 minutes if not kept in a plastic bag and turns to mush if frozen and defrosted. Yes, it makes good toast and is it 'easy' to construct a sandwich from it, in the same way that it is 'easy' to make gravy from granules or bolognaise from a jar. British people rarely eat bread with their meals and in my experience most keep commit the unforgivable sin of keeping it in the fridge so a whole loaf can last a week. By this definition, the British nation does not love bread.

So why, oh why, oh why is it that as soon as a little bit of snow comes around, every British person rushes to the shop and buys 5 loaves and a dozen bread rolls? It amazes me.

Do they suddenly get the urge to eat toast? Or make a bread and butter pudding and a dozen rounds of sandwiches? Are they perplexed at the thought of not being able to make a sandwich for at least a day until the next delivery gets through the snow, despite having a cupboard full of pot-noodles as backup.

What is wrong with people? It's not just bread either, they rush out and buy milk by the tanker load and enough fresh vegetables to make accompany 20 Sunday roasts. Didn't they go shopping last week? Why cant people organise themselves to shop for groceries once a week? At the very worst, in the most rural of areas, villages may be cut off for up to 3 days. In towns, more realistically it could be one day at the most. Thirty years ago, before we all had freezers then shopping only once a week may have been a little harder. But nowadays, surely we can survive for a day.

As the snow falls in this remote village for the second time in a week, I was the fool who didn't buy 10 loaves last week and now I have to visit an empty shop in despair. The lady apologises and says that they still haven't managed to catch up with supplies after last week's panic buying. Maybe I can buy some on ebay? Otherwise, I will just have to eat cake!

Grand Ideas?

December 2010

What is it with that programme Grand Designs? I used to enjoy peoples quirky ideas of a building a fabulous new house with loads of natural light and stunning views. I was even inspired by it when I designed our barn conversion, a 10 metre high wooden structure with a glass front and balcony.

So just when did Kevin McLeod turn into and eco-tit and the program spiral out of control towards the green party? When was it that suddenly the only way to get on the show was to be a complete and utter fruitcake?

On one recent programme, an imbecile decided to build a house he had seen on the back of a yoghurt pot! To make things worse he had absolutely no building experience whatsoever. A water mill, on stilts on the side of a 30 degree slope in the hills with no natural water within 5 miles. What a feckin eejut!?

The show before that a man built one out of straw bales. Great. I used to do that too. When I was 8 years old. I hope he has plenty of eco-friendly rat poison!

People drive 100 miles in a lorry to get three pieces of recycled cardboard to build an internal wall because it is more 'eco-friendly' than plaster board. Never mind the fact that the lorry has just gassed half of the country and used 40 gallons of fuel to fetch it.

And let's put some turf on the roof. What's that about? Who is going up there to mow the lawn?

I know, here's a good idea, lets build a house under ground. What!? Have you seen a mole close too? It can't see because it has had to squint in the dark all its life.

Please get this rubbish off our screens before this man is certified and committed!

Cow Factor

December 2010

It is an ill wind that blows nobody any good. The snowy weather in Scotland has contained me indoors in this old seaside cottage for a good while now. I started by passing the time doing a jigsaw I found in the cupboard. It took me a couple of days. I am quite pleased with that as it said 3-5 years on the box!

The remainder of the time has been allocated to the completion of my second novel which has just been sent off for proofing. The book is called *In the Company of Animals* and picks up with Princess the young cow, the extraordinary character who was central to my first novel, The Right Colour.

The books are now building into a series about Princess and her pals, telling colourful tales of some of their exploits, aimed at a younger audience. In this second book, Princess breaks out of jail along with her two friends, Goliath, a very shy bull, and Jackson, a psychopathic sheep. Their adventures lead them over some tricky terrain when they eventually take shelter with some gypsies and are offered for sale at a large Horse Fair.

I am now well into the third book in this series, entitled *Cow Factor*, when the Princess and her gang get chance to feature on a TV show. There are at least two more books to come in this series which we hope to release for sale in Autumn 2011.

The series may not end there either. As long as I can keep making myself laugh out loud whilst I write them, I hope the end will not be in sight for some time yet.

First class Xmas

December 2010

Yep, we have done it again. Postponed writing out Christmas cards until the very last minute, which means they will now have to be sent first class.

This I year I got round to wondering why we bother. I don't mean to sound a Scrooge (although that is probably what I am) but are Xmas cards really necessary? This year, we are not even at home, so they will pile up in our mailbox until I get chance to pick them up some time in January. And we wont receive any here as nobody knows where we are living.

We bought some really nice ones this year and I am tempted to just write a few to ourselves. *'To us from us, hope you like the card, we chose it specially. Sorry didn't send a present, but we didn't know what you wanted this year.'*

See, if we all did that we would get a few nice cards and look at the money we would save on buying first class stamps at three hundred pounds each. In fact the more organised ones amongst us, you know, the ones who dig the snow from their driveway with tea spoon so they can chug off to work for the government and clutter up the roads. Well they could give themselves theirs early to save money.

We also wouldn't have to queue up at the village Post Office catching germs from all the sniffling people for 3 hours. 3 bloody hours to the only desk that is open because the Post Mistress has caught flu from the people in the queue last week. She is probably sitting at home by the fire writing bloody Christmas cards and watching Jeremy Kyle.

The good old smiling postie wouldn't have to brave the bracing weather and be dug out of snowdrifts by men in fluorescent jackets, delivering illegible hand written envelopes with only half a post code because the sender couldn't be arsed to look it up on line. As always, it makes perfect sense to me.

OK, Merry Christmas everyone!

PS anyone wishing to know our address please email me!

Snow bites

December 2010

Why is it that the media insist on using sensationalist clichés every time we get a smattering of snow.

The country is *gripped* in a big freeze, temperatures will *struggle* to get above freezing. It's called frost, it happens every year because it is winter, just get on with it.

Travel plans in *disarray*, hundreds of travellers stranded. Yes, its winter. Runways need to be cleared of snow. Or would they rather all die in a plane crash.

Main arteries of the country *ground* to a standstill? Because morons run the councils perhaps, and because only morons go out driving in the snow? Shut the roads, clear the snow, open them again? Let the lorries through first. Then the 4x4's. Too much snow, send the drivers back home. Can't get to work? Take a day off. Or even better, use the telephone. Simples.

Turkey shoot

January 2010

Who was it that said 'retrospect' is a thing of the past? Well it was me actually. By the time this goes to print all my memories of Christmas and New Year will be long forgotten. In fact we may even be back in France once more and enjoying an early summer, with lambs frolicking in the meadows. But as we spent the majority of our festive season in Rock this year, I would beg some forgiveness from you if some of it gets a short review in this column this month.

I am sure others will have already mentioned the exceptionally bad weather that the UK experienced in December, with our little cottage in East Scotland catching the brunt of the snow. The vision of the sand dunes a foot deep in snow and even snow on the beach with the waves lapping against it were somewhat bizarre to say the very least. But life goes on, snow melts, hangovers fade, VAT rates increase and the grass grows again as we enter a new year. Not that it's over yet, that is very doubtful. Grandfather always said *"never come March, never come winter"* which I think loosely translates into *"Local councils, don't use up all your road salt until at least April if you want to get voted in again next year!"*

While in the pub over Christmas, which seemed to be all too frequent, Wendy, my better half conspired with the locals that I warranted a haircut. I have to agree that I did, not having had one for well over a year.

I had considered that March may be a good time, when the weather picked up and the French sun was shining. But I was overruled. Pockets, wallets, piggy banks and even whole bank accounts were proffered in the direction of charity, were I to have my head shaved, on New Years Eve, in a public inn. And so it was, December 31st in the Rock Cross, that my ears were once more exposed to the cold. I would like to thank all those who donated money to Midlands Air Ambulance for this cause, particularly those instigators, Tony and Hayden who donated in excess of £100 each. Also a big thanks to Dave and Emma, the pub's new proprietors, for being such a sport. The final total raised was £825 for the charity and a woolly hat for me! I now have a chest infection verging on pneumonia which was possibly brought on as a direct result of this rush of cold air. I am currently bed-ridden as I write. Wouldn't it be ironic if I had to call out the Air Ambulance to lift me to hospital!

I was not the only one to feel a sudden rush of cold air over that period. Whilst in UK we left our few sheep at home in France, to be overlooked occasionally by our good friends and neighbours. What I hadn't reckoned on was lambs being born in our absence. Our ram had lazed about all summer, not showing any interest in sex during the hot days and as a result we were not expecting lambs until March. Well all I can think is that he must have perked up under the hours of darkness during July as two lambs were born to the world on Christmas day. To make matters somewhat worse, their birth coincided with an uncharacteristic bout of bad weather. A gambling man may have placed a bet on a white Xmas in Aberdeen at 3-1, Edinburgh at 4-1 or possibly the Midlands at 6-1. What he may have shied away from was South-West France at 400-1. But yep, that's where it fell, 6 inches on Christmas morning. In hindsight, I should have bet our house on it, but then in hindsight I wouldn't have entrusted this year's lambing to two kind-hearted folk with no more experience in that subject than I have in brain surgery. I heartily thank Josie and Stu for their help in my irresponsible absence. Mary and Joseph are doing fine!

The other day I had a play on a Wii games console with an excellent new game where you got chance to shoot at flying turkeys on your TV with a special toy gun that was provided. Although the game was great fun I got round to considering that wouldn't it be even better if the inventors added a few enhancements for this model which would allow you to shoot at actual TV programmes! For starters every time the adverts came on I would fell those two moustachioed 118 idiots and follow up by taking out that annoying singer on the Go-Compare advert. Now we're talking turkey! And what about that stupid woman on 'I'm a Celebrity Get Me Out of Here'? The one who had a phobia about insects? Bang bang, you're out of here now! And Ant and Dec as well come to think of it. I could flick through the channels and pick-off Anne Robinson, Jeremy Kyle, then that dreadful man on Strictly Come Dancing with the fake Italian accent. I could even put old Brucie out of his misery too. They would need to adapt a rapid-fire version so I could wipe out the whole cast of Eastenders in 20 seconds and I would finish with a highly satisfying shot into Jonathan Ross, just below the waist! Hours of fun from my own armchair. Some come-on Nintendo, invent the Wii 'TV Assassin' in time for my Xmas next year. I am saving up for it already.

Whilst on the subject of flying turkeys I would like to question the accuracy of public surveys. Sorry to pick on the Welsh yet again this month but a snippet from a survey was sent to me as follows:

'ONE in five Welsh people believe that turkeys can fly while just over one in 10 are convinced the bird originates from Turkey, according to the findings of a new survey.'

Now the contents of this survey may be quite startling and slightly embarrassing to the Welsh nation were it not for the inclusion of the next line which says:

'..the poll quizzed over 150 people about their festive eating....'

So that's 151 people out of an entire population, hardly a cross section one must admit. But what it doesn't say is who these people are or where they were? Nursery children maybe? Outside a psychiatric hospital per chance? Incidentally, I believe turkeys can fly too. Some can, can't they? They certainly used to in olden days before they got so fat.

During my spare time in the Autumn I penned a biography about my father, John Frazier, which I then gave him as a Xmas present. I was a little apprehensive about how it would be received as not all the facts were one hundred percent accurate. I need not have worried as he was very appreciative and even a little touched that someone had taken time to recognise some of his life achievements and present them in a readable way. However he was a little bit bemused when I said I might offer a few copies for sale. "Who would want to buy stories about me?" he said. Well it seems that quite a few people do actually and copies are going fast. All profits of the sale of this will go to Midlands Air Ambulance. Called *"I use my thumbs as a yardstick"*, the book is available online at www.andyfrazier.co.uk or behind the bar in his local pub, the Rock Cross.

Incidentally I just discovered that *"dammit I'm mad"* spelled backwards is *"dammit I'm mad"*. Does this mean that even dyslexic mad people have no excuse? I wonder.

A brief glimpse of home.

January 2010

I have made a quick trip back to France this week, for a few reasons. A combo of Ryan and EJ got me here, screaming as ever. It seems they have moved the usual flight gate in Stanstead from 40 to 39. They are at least a mile apart. In different counties. I just make my flight and get seated next to the mad woman who endows me with her life story whilst I frantically try to read the Metro for comfort. I make it to our home, flick on the electric heater and kettle. Then fumble for the trip switch, which throws a tantrum, on my way to a welcome but cold bed.

Next morning, a meeting with a man who needs to provide us with a survey of our soil so I can install a new Fosse Septique (septic tank). He needs to provide some extra thickness to the already massive pile of paperwork that has evolved since our original application 2 years ago. Well soil is a loose term for the ground our house sits on. In fact it is not just built on it but OF it, as is possibly some of our crockery. This is the same stuff on that potters wheel scene in Ghost. Only stickier.

A smiley young man arrives in a statutory white van, spends 2 hours digging holes. I suggest that he may want to dig the vegetable patch and plant my earlies while he is at it. But low and behold, he has a sense of humour and a good understanding of English. I speak to him only in French. I have come all this way to see him, the least he can do is honour me by using the native language! As it happens, he turns out to be the Messiah; our 'terre' has a reasonable level of permeability and it will be possible for me to use a lateral draining system without the need to build a pit full of a thousand tons of sand. All this discussed in French. Impressed? Well I was as it has probably just saved us a couple of grand.

The second reason for the visit was to check over the place. It was cold, damp and full of wildlife. And that's just inside the house. I lit the fire and kept it in for two days. As luck would have it, the ceilings have caved in due to excessive damp. Waste not want not, the pile of wood and mouse droppings lying on and around the bed in the back bedroom helped with the heating. A good policy. If your house falls down in winter, put it on the fire.

Reason three was to check out our new arrivals in the shape of four lambs. All seem OK, but I'm not sure that one of the ewes will manage to milk enough to rear her two offspring. I let them out into the garden and my golf course! Plenty of grass there. An electric fence will contain them in that section. I erect it in beautiful sunshine that fries the early frost from the ground. Winter is short here and the already lengthening days remind me of a Scottish May day.

I also popped into to see my neighbouring farmer to ask him for another bale of hay for the hungry beasts. He made me a coffee, using instant coco and tap water! Then that was washed down with something from a bottle on which the only thing I could decipher was 45% proof. From Spain. It tasted like cough medicine. Except it worked on the legs not the chest. Mine felt as light as air when I left!

Now a seat by the fire is my evening position. The house is as draught-free as an international draughts convention, but there is something satisfying about burning parts of your house to warm your knees. The insurance company may not agree. The wood spits and crackles like a winter Bastille day display. The fire proof rug no longer has any pile left to burn. The same can be said for my slippers.

But a trip down to the cave provides me with a rather nice Bordenave Madiran, 2005. It is gorgeous and a refreshing change after 6 weeks of enduring Aussie end-of-bin or Chilean mountain-goats-piss in UK. Some Toulouse sausages in the pan, cooked in Dijonaise sauce add to the bliss. That and no TV.

Yes I am enjoying the two month time in our Scottish centrally heated cottage by the sea, but there is still only one Chez Nous and its is 2000 miles south of there.

I leave tomorrow. Just as well, I am running out of firewood. The Ikea chairs would be next and I am not sure they are insured.

What does God do?

January 22nd 2010

I was baptised when I was an infant, nothing to do with religion, more to do with society. At school I went to confirmation classes, totally oblivious about what was being confirmed, by whom, to whom. All I knew was, at 13, we got free wine and skived off from prep.

I then spent 20 years married to an RE teacher, brought my children up as Christians and went to church at least monthly. During most of this time I had an element of confusion. God who? What about Darwin, Muslims, Cot Death? I never really gave it too much thought. To me, Man and Boy, God was God. He spurred jokes, caused wars and generally demanded money.

When we lost a son, still-born, a priest came and comforted us. He didn't really take away any pain. He couldn't, that was God's job. God didn't really help either.

The very same God let my fabulous brother-in-law die, he and the NHS. Aged 51. I asked him why, I reckoned I was entitled to do that? A 22 year old priest tried to help, but couldn't.

So today, when my only sister, my strong healthy steadfast rock of a beautiful sister gets struck down, for no apparent reason, should I call God again?

As I sit on this bleak night, for hours watching her heart beat in green peaks on a screen, should I pray?

Should I ask for something from this God who has given me some free wine and yet let me down so badly before? I will ask him, I have to. For the only person in the world I would exchange my life for, would die for, is my sis. If you can do it, I say, then do it now. I don't really have a subscription, no real faith, just hope.

I know about hope and I believe in the power of belief too. *"I think, therefore I am"*, that is philosophy. *"My god is better than your god, and if you say different I will kill you for it"*, that is religion.

If she, my big lovely sister, comes though this should I thank God? Become a believer, get down on my knees? I do believe she will get through it. Medical magic and her formidable strength will underpin that. Is that down to God too?

If she dosent, which she will, but if she doesn't, can I tell God, the Almighty, that he fucked up yet again. The priest, now 23, will tell me that God gave her a good life. Bollocks, she is fifty fucking one, that's all. And she he already took her husband and soul-mate. He may say that God moves in mysterious ways. You can say that again, he sure got me baffled and I aint stupid. I can understand rules of most things, even back-gammon. So, this God fucker, isn't it time he showed up now? Showed his hand? Come on Man, Ace are trumps and you hold all the cards.

I gave up on Santa and the tooth fairy a long time ago, and **you** I never knew. But help me now and I will find out what you really do all day. Because you or nobody else has the right to take my sister from me. Bring her back. Intact. OK? And then I will restore some faith and, when I have to, I will pay.

Farmhouse outpost

January 2010

The internet and mobile communications have revolutionised our personal and business lives. *Discuss*.

It has now been just over a week since my sister had a severe brain haemorrhage that was extremely close to taking her life. That week has been nothing short of sheer hell. I was warned it may be a roller-coaster ride and that we all should hang on tight as her condition buffets us forwards, backwards and sideways. It has certainly done that in spades. 2 operations, prolonged coma, high risks of strokes, and absolute uncertainly have all added their degree of stress. The counterbalance to that has been formidable doctors, surgeons, nurses and facilities. I have to admit total admiration for the new Queen Elisabeth hospital in Birmingham, not just for its amazing modern architecture but for all its staff. We are not out of the woods yet and have been warned it may be months before we see any real progress from her current state. I and just about everyone else will gladly take that as a good result.

However, for the last week I have assumed the role of go-between. The project manager if you will, liaising with doctors, nurses, children, parents, friends, pets and family in a bid to keep everyone informed of progress and on the visiting rota. Not a problem, I am quite comfortable in that role, it keeps me busy and challenges me.

The real problem I do have is that I have been staying with my parents, both in their eighties, at the old farmhouse. This house not only does not have internet access, it also has very limited mobile phone coverage. To add to the problem, most of the rooms, including the one we are sleeping in, still have round-pin plugs! There are probably only a few people who even remember these things which were phased on in the seventies to be replaced with the square ones the rest of have now. They stopped selling adaptors from square to round about 30 years ago. This is itself is very inconvenient, especially as I am trying my best to communicate to in excess of 100 people requiring updates on Sarah's condition. As I am first point of call in an emergency, it has also been difficult to ensure that I am contactable 24/7. Mobile phones require charging. But I have managed and, with Wendy's support, we are still managing, albeit somewhat displaced from our own comfort zones.

We eat out every night as the cooker only has one gas ring, which is lit from a match. Also the gas oven frequently goes out which is slightly alarming. The house does have a TV, which is unable to show anything except films pre 1950, mostly starring John Wayne. Likewise, the radio only plays classical music in between adverts for mobility scooters and Zimmer frames, very loudly. The phone line is crackly, possibly still run on copper wire.

99% of the houses in rural France are more up to date than din of antiquity. All this would be extremely quaint were it not for my immediate need for enough technology to fulfil my liaising role, but I am not complaining, just coping.

What I do find incredible is that the family farm is still run from this outpost. Without internet in this day and age? Is it any wonder that Tesco buys all their food from overseas?

Broadband has now been ordered, but that will take a month to install. A month? Good old BT? So only one thing for it, I am about to order 500 carrier pigeons and keep them in the granary. Anyone know of a good website I can buy them from?

Queen Elisabeth's biscuits

February 2010

Yet another interesting month in the life of a simple soul. A few quiet days after New Year, nursing my freezing ears, afforded me some time to enjoy a bit more of our Scottish surroundings. For a short while the weather picked up and some brisk walks with the dogs on the beach were a welcome change. I even took time to entertain myself by doing a jigsaw I found in the cupboard. It only took me a couple of days. I was quite pleased, it said 3-5 years on the box!

On the good news front, the hair is now growing back after last months scalping, albeit a wee bit greyer than I was hoping for.

Then, from nowhere I get a phone call bringing bad tidings. More family issues, this time my sister in intensive care. I won't include all the details, other than she is still fighting on, but for a while the odds were stacked well against her survival. Having lost her husband last year, life can be very unfair sometimes. Things like this certainly make you sit up and appreciate life.

When I was nineteen, my uncle died suddenly aged 60. He had worked hard all his life and amassed enough money to retire in luxury but sadly he never got chance to move into his lovely house on the south coast. A month later, I lost a close friend of my own age. At that young age, I made a few decisions. I was well aware of hard work but I also realised that work had to be fun, life had to be fun, because on that day I realised it could be taken away from you in an instant. I am no prophet or church minister with a point to prove, but from my current stand point, I thank my old uncle for inadvertently giving me that advice. People who proffer the words *"life is too short"* are those who have enough time to think about it. The ones who really advocate that statement are too busy cramming as much into their life as possible and enjoying every day as a result. Sure, when you are busy, life goes by faster, but if you are busy doing what you enjoy, logic says you should get more enjoyment from life. Here endeth the lesson, except to say thanks to all those who have privately and publicly prayed for Sarah and for all the good wishes received. We believe that she may now be on the road to a slow recovery.

There *have* been a few high points this month, England beating Wales in the 6 nations for example. The man from the French water board passing our planning application for a new septic tank at last. The remainder of our ewes lambing in France without aid. However, for the next few months I may exchange my rantings from a French farmhouse to those from a more temporary location as I endeavour to stay near my sister to help with her recovery.

But the rantings will go on, continually, for tis my job. Last week on the way for a hospital visit, we purchased a large packet of dog biscuits. A conundrum then arose. It is fairly obvious that we are unable to take our dogs in for hospital visits, but would we be allowed to take the dog biscuits in instead? If not they would be devoured by Louis (the pointless pointer) waiting eagerly in the car. As she is prone to do, Wendy came up with a sensible solution; we should put the packet under the car out of sight and collect them on our return an hour later. A *wise* woman, I hear you say. What she hadn't reckoned on was that Birmingham, unlike south west France, is inhabited by thieves and charlatans. To our dismay, on our return, someone had stolen the packet of biscuits from us, a feat that would have involved crawling on their belly under the vehicle! Louis was heartbroken, how could anyone be so cruel to deprive him of his dinner? I was more intrigued as to who would be so desperate to stoop so low. Was it a fellow dog owner, surely not, they would have spotted our dogs in the car? Or a hungry homeless person surviving on canine food ? Or even another large dog on the scavenge? Only our dogs or the cctv cameras can tell us that. So maybe it will turn up on police 5 next week. Does Shaw Taylor still present Police 5, or I am showing my age?

It has been a while since I have travelled into south Birmingham and it was with a wry smile that I noticed Longbridge has now all but disappeared. That hub of manufacturing, once the car building centre of Europe, reduced to brown fields awaiting reconstruction. On closer inspection, I note the much of the planned new construction is for education premises and yet more universities. That plus the infinite extension of the cities other two universities is a massive ongoing project, probably using foreign contractors. But who is going to pay for all this building I ask? Well you and me (alright not me, I live in France, but certainly you), the tax payer.

Does anyone else see the irony here? Kids in that area would have left school at 16 and worked at Longbridge, learning something useful, making something useful (well as useful as a Rover could be) and earning money. Now they leave university at 22, with degrees in 'work-avoidance' and remain unemployed for 3 more years, at our expense. Here's a theory, Mr Cameron. Encourage the kids to leave school at 16 and learn a trade by going to work building universities. A simple and recursive solution. Soon you will have a land full of empty universities. Then you could charge overseas students to use them. That would pay the bills. You could even put the excess money into good use, like funding NHS and perhaps the Air Ambulance, so that I don't have to get an annual head shave! Incidentally, their services were used recently to take Keyleigh Butcher to the Birmingham hospital from Rock in 6 minutes which is truly astounding. I hope she is recovering from her accident and I am glad my locks went to a good cause!

I would like to finish this month by congratulating the NCC unit in Birmingham QE Hospital for their outstanding service and thank them for all the help they have given my sister. I know the NHS comes under regular fire, but I can only speak as I find and they have been nothing short of brilliant. Bravo.

Don't commandeer the common deer

February 2010

What on earth does the government think its doing selling off our forests? Yes, there are some examples of how privatisation of national assets has been a worked reasonably well in the past. Well, privatisation of sorts. More specifically, private companies running national assets with government funding. The NHS, car parking, the car industry, the rail network...? Actually no, there are not any examples of privatisation of national assets working well at all are there? They are all crap.

So why would the forests be any different? For instance, who would pay for all the fencing needed to keep people out of these lovely wooded areas? Because, if a private company buys a forest, it would surely want to charge folks to use it for, say, bird watching, dog walking etc. We would be expected to enter via turnstile and hand over our cash to a spotty pale faced vegan in exchange for a map of the muddy paths, with pictures helping us indentify blue tits, bluebells and edible mushrooms. Power crazed police wardens would roam the woods, competing for commission for penalties to be handed out to those who broke the rules. Wheel clamping would be in operation for not only our cars, but prams and bikes too. Fines would be handed out for dogs that barked, children that screamed and anyone who went for a tinkle behind a tree. In short, the government would expect the forests to be like their cities. Car-less and controlled by CCTV in operation.

But what concerns me more is the animals. Will they be privatised too? Can you buy a squirrel? Are they able to sell off our deer and wild boar? Because if you fence the people out then, by contrast, you sure fence the animals in? What if a couple of deer had gone off on an away-day while the fences were being erected and returned at midnight to find themselves separated from their families? It would be like Berlin in the 1950's. In 30 years time, the fences would come down during some mass demonstration and the "free" deer would be queuing up to visit long forgotten relatives still living in hovels.

Or here is another theory, they could install animal turnstiles too. So the privatised animals would be allowed out at certain times as long as they were home by midnight. It would be like South Africa. Perhaps the owls would be trained as spies or wardens. The odd animals would escape and live as fugitives, being constantly followed and tracked down by the CIA and the Daily Star. In years to come, a bird verses quadruped hatred would evolve and eventually evolution would encourage four legged animals to grow wings.

You see, Mr Conservative minister, nature is something that happens outside Whitehall. Evolution may change the colour of your government, but mess with nature, you are messing with God, The Farmer and the Sunday Roast.

Good honest rant

March 2010

Anyone who has been to Worcester lately will know, to their detriment, that there is maintenance being done on Holt Fleet bridge at present. So could someone please explain to me why the two traffic lights, one at either end of the bridge, require to be 'manned'. When I say manned, I mean overseen by a rather unintelligent and bored looking chap watching the queuing vehicles, wearing a hard hat. A hard hat when he is nowhere near the building site? For what purpose exactly? Perhaps it is in case the traffic light falls on his head? Maybe a plane passing overhead might inadvertently drop a wheel or a peanut from the sky? No, we all know the real reason? It is yet another example of health and safety taken to a ridiculous level. The man is employed by building firm, hard hat compulsory, despite him being in no danger whatsoever, these are rules, black and white. Except, of course, if he wishes to wear a turban instead like one of his colleagues. But that is another issue entirely.

While on the subject of mysteries, could anyone enlighten me about the road sign at the entrance to the Birmingham hospital. It reads: '*No entry, except for access.*' Why else would anyone want to enter if not for access? Access to what? Perhaps I would like to enter, do a little dance in the middle of the road again, and then leave without actually accessing the hospital? At least it is written in English, unlike some of the other signs around that district. Oops, there goes my xenophobic streak again.

I have very little interest in football and even less understanding of the game. However, it seems that the thuggish image it portrays has yet reached another highlight. I open the paper to see Wayne Crooney (names changed to protect the ..etc) has recently punched someone in the face, only to be allowed to play in a match the next day, unpunished. Even more of a dismay, one of the players on the opposing side has recently shot someone with an air rifle. The fact that the team is owned by a Mafia don has either gone unnoticed by the press or they are too afraid to make the connection. What next? The prevalent use of flick-knives for all premiership strikers to be sanctioned by the FA? Perhaps the goalie should be armed with an AK47? Is it any wonder that there is so much violence on the streets? As said, I have little knowledge of the game but did hear a rather amusing joke on the subject, possibly made by a rugby fan: When Ashley Cole shot that student with an air rifle, Didier Drodber rolled around on the ground pretending to be injured. I guess to some this may be funny although somewhat lost on me!

I couldn't rant this month without a mention of that good old dictator, Colonel Mu-ammar Gadaffi. Possibly, by the time this goes to print, he may be no longer with us, in fact by the time I finish this sentence he could well have been terminated! He makes speeches saying: "my people love me....!" Ahem, and which people are these exactly? The ones he has ordered his army to shoot at per chance. The ones who are fleeing the country? The ones who are rioting to depose him after 40 years of oppression? And to think that after the carnage of the Lockerbie aircraft bombings we, the UK, has since been doing business with this maniac? My online blog carries the heading that *"the lunatics have taken over the asylum..!"*. I usually proffer this line somewhat tongue-in-cheek but this man really is one lunatic too many. Maybe we should send one of our football players to sort him out!

Having written this column for just over two years now, it would be remiss of me not to mention the annual battle of rugby that our nation has with the French this time of year, the result being 2 wins to one in our favour during that time. Shame I wasn't in France this year on that winning occasion to wind up my neighbours once more. It is normally the only day of the year when the St Georges flag flies at chez nous and, dammit, I missed it!

Talking of rugby, the flags are still flying half mast in that home of the game, Christchurch, New Zealand. Having visited the city some years ago, with another trip planned this autumn, it was shocking to see footage of buildings and the cathedral falling to the ground. Thankfully, the few friends I have over there are all OK, but it certainly has rocked the country emotionally as well as physically. My heart goes out to those with friends and relatives caught up in the disaster. It is still our intention to go there in September, albeit the rugby games we were going to watch may be rescheduled elsewhere.

I was in France briefly this month to sort of some business. While checking on the sheep, I discovered that our head count has increased by one. A wandering minstrel of a ram has taken up residence amongst our flock, but from where he came I have no idea as there are no other sheep around us for miles. I considered keeping him but then, as I listened, I heard the very faint sound of a guillotine being sharpened in the village. Seemingly the death penalty is still in force for sheep rustling in France, especially if you are English, and particularly if your nation has just beaten the home nation at their national sport. So, in by best French, I declared the beast to the local Mairie in some sort of bizarre French amnesty. The poor chap was quite confused as I attempted to describe to the creature in a combination of pigeon-French and sign language. "Un grand mouton monsieur" said I, waving my arms, "avec les grand ballons..!" I think he considered phoning me a doctor!

Someone the other day described my rantings as a bit "Clarksonesque"; another of those new adjectives that never found its way in Samuel Johnson's original Oxford dictionary. I am not sure if this was a compliment or an insult but I was hasty to point out the difference between the great J Clarkson and myself. He is a foot taller than me for one thing. He is also infinitely more wealthy, witty and famous. On the other hand, I do have a little more chance of avoiding slander and libel cases than he does. For instance, if I was to say that all Mexicans are lazy good-for-nothing so-and-so's with droopy moustaches or what ever accusation he made on Top Gear, I would be far less lightly to be taken to task by the Mexican government for mentioning it in R&DN. I will not, of course, make those accusations at all. I met a Mexican once, he was a nice chap. Or was he Brazilian? Definitely from one of those peasant filled South American bandit countries anyway.

But herein hangs a point. TV and radio gets scrutinised by all and sundry and the BBC is forced to adhere to something near the truth. Whereas the press…well don't get me started. How can they continually get away with printing blatant lies and half-truths just to sell newspapers, with no recompense whatsoever? I actually have adopted the attitude of believing the opposite of whatever I read in daily print to be the truth. With the exception of this quality magazine, obviously.

Anyway, I digress. This week, on a trip back from London, I encountered my first four pound sandwich. That's a heavy meal, I hear you say. But no, this was not in weight but in money. Yes, the meagre sandwich has finally reached the four quid threshold. So it was, and this is where I feel I can name and shame, unlike the great JC, that I pulled into a service station called Welcome Break. Is it any wonder I was 'Welcome' when they charge prices like that? And 'broke' I surely would be if I visited them too frequently. So let's make a quick analysis here. Two slices of bread – 10p, a slice of dry cooked chicken – 5p, some lettuce and mayo – 2p. Total cost less than 20p? And packaging, you say? Well I don't want the packaging thanks, I can't eat that. Or maybe it tastes as good as the product inside? What I found really preposterous was that the company who makes said sandwich has the slogan "Good Honest Food!" What the..? Where is the honesty in charging four quid for a sarnie? How honest is making 2000% profit in this day an age? Yes it had travelled all the way from Cornwall. Bully for it. It could have travelled by first class rail with its own private carriage complete with hand-maidens and en-suite butter-bath and still been cheaper! It is nothing short of an outrage. When cigarettes reached the one pound per pack threshold, I gave them up. Should I now consider giving up sandwiches too? Or at the very least I should revert to rolling my own.

Wellies on the ground floor.

March 2010

And so it is that we move house once again. This will be the 15th house I have lived in. Most people live in two or possibly three all their lives. I suppose that classes me as some sort of nomad. It's 3am. A cup of tea has calmed my nerves after waking in a cold sweat.

This is a tiny cottage by the river, idyllic you could say, nice and cozy for us two and the dogs. Walkies by the river, no less than 16 friendly pubs to drop into, a few nice bistros and a couple of Indian restaurants. It is also handy for the hospital where my poor sister still lies, allowing me continue my daily visits.

But here is the trap. The dogs are not allowed above the ground floor, we have signed a contract on their behalf to ensure this. I say we signed it, Wendy and I signed it, they didn't. So poor Louis cannot understand why, after four years of access all areas, he is confined to the kitchen.

And the problem doesn't stop there. You see this little cottage is in a small town called Bewdley and the little river outside the door is none other than the notorious River Severn. I say notorious, as many will recognise the name because every time we have a period of prolonged rain in middle England, the river Severn (to coin a cliché from the journalists here) *bursts its banks*, right outside our door. Fortunately, for the good people of Bewdley, flood defences were installed in this town a few years ago which now protect it from the worst of the carnage that flood water can bring. But that still relies on the council getting them in place, in time. My biggest worry is where do they get their weather forecast from? For instance, do they sit and watch "hopeless the weathergirl" blather on in her dimwit way on channel 4 each evening? Or do they get their information from the met-office, you know that over paid bunch of tossers who occasionally look out of the window to tell us its raining. The ones who couldn't forecast a barn door banging in a gale. Possibly the council use a crystal ball or a time machine to make their predictions? It is all a worry.

Thankfully, this is a three story cottage, so we would expect to be reasonably safe were it that Noah was summoned to the fore at a moments notice. But what about those poor dogs, the ones we signed a contract for?

Let the nightmares begin. All last night I endured that recurring one where I wake up and see two defenceless pooches floating down the high street still asleep in their beds. Perhaps I should complain to the RSPCA? Or at least buy them some wellies and waterwings.

Who wants to know?

The day we moved into this little cottage coincided with the 2011 census form falling on the new doormat. I opened and had a laugh as did many households. 'Do you speak English?' No, can you send me a form written in German? 'This question is intentionally left blank'....One assumes they had forgotten the question they were intending to ask!

What I find quite confusing is the ethnic question. It seems one can no longer settle for being British. I have always been British and quite proud of it. The fact that I don't live permanently in Britain is my choice. The fact that I don't live in Britain also, I believe, exemplifies me from filling in the illiterate rubbish anyway. Am I breaking the law? Well catch me if you can, because if I don't fill it in, you won't know where I live!

When it comes to Rugby, yes I support England because that is where I was born. But does that make me English? I don't want to be English, I have met a lot of English people in France and I don't like many of them. My grandmother was Welsh, does that make me Welsh? After all, my brother supports Wales in the 6 nations. But, on the whole, I dislike the Welsh as well. My surname, Frazier, suggests I am possibly from Scottish ancestry or perhaps French. My mother's maiden name, McCormick, definitely originates from Southern Ireland. Do I have the right to decide what nationality I am? And if so, can I reserve my right not to tell anyone?

Because, to be frank, what the f**k does it have to do with them? I understand that the Doomsday book was necessary so that the new King on the block could work out exactly what it was he had just won. When tracing my own ancestors, I did refer to the 1881 census which fed me dome useful information, I agree. But if I fill in this one, I will give the government a bum steer because I am only living here for 2 months, I would rather be in France and I don't want to be tagged by nationality or religion. Where is the question, 'Do you like living in England?' So I can answer 'No, I think it is a shithole and the government are a bunch of overpaid tossers! They didn't ask me that one, did they? Maybe that is the one that was intentionally left blank?

This is what I think will happen. This information will be used for the wrong reasons. Statistics will show that certain areas now have ethnic majorities and this will be used to fuel the uprising that is spreading from the middle east into some of our cities. Britain is sitting on an ethnic time-bomb and once all this information gets collated it will only help it tick a little faster. There, I have said what others dare not to and for that reason I am not about to tell anyone where I live.

About the author

Andy Frazier is mainly an author of children's stories. Occasionally he writes things for grown ups too but he finds this quite hard as he has never quite grown up himself. He has always wanted to write ever since he was a child and now he can't think of anything he would rather do. He gets his most enjoyment out of creating colourful characters and then bringing them to life in humorous situations.

History

Born into a life of farming, it took a long time and a lot of determination to get away from it, but he thinks he has just about achieved that now. Andy did quite a few things during his career, including agricultural contracting, retail sales, sheep breeding and IT before he somehow became a business analyst working in a city. Oh yes, and at one time he was an expert in grooming cows. It all made sense at the time.

One day, he had a eureka moment and upped sticks to South West France. He now lives there on a smallholding where he shares his time equally between his partner, some more sheep, some DIY tools and a set of golf clubs. Despite all the obvious distractions that renovating a big old farmhouse presents, Andy spends most of his mornings writing and that is the bit he enjoys most.